Right Woman, Right Now!

Right Woman, Right Now!

THE FOOLPROOF
GUIDE TO GETTING
THE GIRL YOU WANT

Paul Kerton

PIATKUS

Visit the Piatkus website!

Piatkus publishes a wide range of best-selling fiction and non-fiction, including books on health, mind, body & spirit, sex, self-help, cookery, biography and the paranormal.

If you want to:

- read descriptions of our popular titles
- buy our books over the Internet
- take advantage of our special offers
- enter our monthly competition
- learn more about your favourite Piatkus authors

VISIT OUR WEBSITE AT: www.piatkus.co.uk

First published in Great Britain in 2005 by
Piatkus Books Ltd
5 Windmill Street
London W1T 2JA
e-mail: info@piatkus.co.uk

A catalogue record for this book is
available from the British Library

ISBN 0 7499 2536 1

Designed by Briony Chappell
Set in 12pt Minion by
Action Publishing Technology Ltd, Gloucester
Printed and bound in Great Britain by
Antony Rowe Ltd, Chippenham, Wiltshire

To my very own right woman, Tziona.

Contents

Preface

Before you find the right woman you will go through many wrong women – enjoy the ride.

How often have you spotted your 'right woman' across a room and let her get clean away because of a moment's hesitation, spawned by inhibition or lack of confidence? We've all been there – you're consumed with desire for this one woman but by the time you whip up the courage, the chutzpah or personal style to approach her and make her yours, she's gone. Out of your life for ever before she even became part of it.

I know exactly what you're thinking – how are you ever going to find and secure your *right woman* when you can't even bring yourself to approach *any* woman, never mind *that* one woman of your dreams? You wouldn't know what to say if you did and haven't got a clue how to move things on seamlessly from that initial casual contact to a first date, first kiss and successful seduction.

Look, I know what you're thinking because I've been there. It may have been a while but I still remember those initial crippling fears – of rejection, of ridicule, and other self-imposed psychological obstacles that we men have to overcome before we shake that emotional 'double six' to get in the game, refine our technique and enter the realm of 'experienced' with women.

I know that sense of longing to connect with that special woman and that hollow emptiness when you disappoint yourself and chicken out at the last minute. Or that rabbit-in-the-headlights shock when you come face to face with the woman you've been thinking about every hour of the day. It can be excruciatingly intimidating and seriously debilitating, although you'll find this surprisingly easy to overcome once you acquire the knack.

When, like me, you're not much taller than Tom Cruise (5' 8") without his boyish, white-toothed grin, star appeal or bank balance, then the dating game can seem quite a hostile, one-sided affair and capturing the heart of Princess No.1 seems like Mission Impossible. At school I kept missing out on the best-looking girls who always seemed to be on the arm of somebody else. Being fair, short and 'interesting' poses quite a challenge initially, particularly to a female audience weaned on fairy tales where the prince is always tall, dark and handsome.

At first I worked on my strength which was the fact that I was sporty and hot at soccer and rugby, seeking out equally sporty babes. But the attraction of a nifty overhead kick pales rapidly as the social scene becomes more sophisticated and competitive. Then I realised that the best-looking women didn't always go out with the best-looking men – they tended to go out with those men who made an effort and asked them out first. I was always shy with girls until I decided that enough was enough and I started to push myself and ask girls out first. The more I confronted my fears and engaged with the women around me, the easier it got and the more success I had.

Meeting, engaging and seducing women is a skill as tangible as hitting a good golf drive. There is a knack. Some guys just have it from birth, the rest of us have to work at it, but it isn't *that* difficult with a little practice. What's interesting is that once you tune in to the right wavelength and start giving off the right signals, women start to come to you.

I spent much of my career working on magazines such as *Cosmopolitan* and *Company*, and writing for other national and international women's magazines. What this did was get me closer to the inner core of what women are really all about, and what they really think and feel about men. It was like being a fly on the wall of a women's club, watching and listening to their thoughts about, and reactions to, us men. It was a real eye-opener and gave me terrific insight into the complexities of the modern woman, which I now pass on to you in *Right Woman, Right Now*. The irony is that these supercharged modern women are essentially looking for the same thing we are and are equally nervous about finding it.

I'm not going to lie to you and tell you that all you have to do is read this book and women will fall at your feet. Yes, they will fall, but you will need to put in some groundwork – to take up the challenge, alter your thinking, sharpen up your presentation and make it happen. I'm giving you the ammunition with hundreds of workable, practical tips, insights and strategies to ensure you're equipped to face *any* woman, but I can't be there to ask her out for you. You've got to adapt what I'm telling you to your own style and persona, add your own twist and then get out there.

The dating game is a complex minefield and natural selection is a brutal process, but *Right Woman, Right Now* will arm you with the right skills and that crucial sense of timing you need to date and seduce *that* woman you've been dreaming about or lusting after.

The more success you achieve the better you get at it and the more your confidence soars. Once you've been out with the best girl on campus or the hottest babe in the building, it doesn't matter how long or short the relationship is – you will learn from the experience and you know that once you've done it, you can do it again.

Good luck out there.
Paul Kerton

Introduction

Ever been somewhere really beautiful on your own? St Mark's Square in Venice when the string quartets are playing on a warm summer's evening? Or watched a breathtaking sunset at Key West, or Crete, or simply been away on business and stayed in a luxury 5-star hotel where the bed is the size of a football field and the jacuzzi is an Olympic pool?

If you have then you must know that terrible, empty feeling that the whole situation seems such a wasted opportunity and that you're missing something big in your life. Why do you feel so hollow and empty? Because it's better to share those special moments with somebody you care about.

There's a woman out there with your name etched into her

breast. She's the one with the welcoming smile that understands where you're coming from and where you're heading. She makes you feel completely at ease and allows you to be yourself. She laughs at your jokes, or at least, your personal brand of humour. She shares your interests and accommodates your idiosyncrasies and irritations.

You'll recognise her immediately, the moment you finally find her – but the thing is, where the hell is she? And how do you get to know her? Will you ever kiss her or make love to her? And will you even know it's her when you find her, given that we spend so little time on that initial ice-breaking interchange?

Being successful with women is not a magical, wand-waving sleight-of-hand exercise; and beware of those get-rich-quick books that promise that you can 'seduce *any* woman in ten minutes'. Nine times out of ten it boils down to pure hard work and putting in the required effort. Be sure that while you are not out there working on that beautiful woman with your name engraved on her heart, somebody else is. It's an incredibly competitive market but if you read *Right Woman, Right Now* you'll get the insider knowledge and short cuts you need to get ahead and stay ahead of the pack.

Only you can make it happen and if you don't you'll just sink deeper and deeper into that negative spiral of personal mediocrity: should have, could have, would have … but didn't. Your life will become a catalogue of 'if only' and 'I wish'. Wake up and get with the programme. Get out there and carve a niche for yourself. Start by reading *Right Woman, Right Now*, and you will find your *right woman*.

Even seasoned 'players' can lose their touch or have a 'bad' season like a ten-million-pound striker who hasn't scored in six games, or an opening batsman whose batting average is so low he's developing webbed feet and a beak. That's when we require a refresher course and need to find new inspiration to climb out of the rut of only dating one type of woman, or frequenting one type of place, or using one style of approach.

The dating game is full of false promises and snippets of localised bad advice founded on folklore and cliché; the general consensus is that once you 'get them [i.e. women] between the sheets' then they're all the same. How wrong can that be? Every woman is so different from the next. Also, know this, before you can get a modern woman horizontal you need to spend a large amount of time being impressively vertical and this is what millions of men find to be the tricky part. It isn't just you who stumbles over what to say, how to react and that match-winning ploy of knowing precisely when to make a move – too soon and you've blown it; too late and she's moved on.

What *Right Woman, Right Now* will do is give you a better understanding of your sexual self and the type of woman you should be chasing, as well as hundreds of tips and key strategies on how to release the power of you – and better understand women, engage with them and seduce them. Making the best of what you've got in order to find, and secure, your *right woman, right now*.

National disgrace

I read a damning piece in the *Spectator*, no less, about how British men are useless with women, written by Leah McLaren, an attractive young Canadian arts columnist for the *Globe and Mail* (a Canadian daily newspaper). This 29-year-old blonde with a pretty face but high forehead and thin hair (meow!) apparently came over to the UK on an extended stay and dated a dozen British men, all of whom, she claimed, were completely useless at seduction.

Even Oscar-winning actress Gwyneth Paltrow had a go at

the British male and his seduction technique by complaining that nobody had asked her out during her time in London, and moaning about how useless we all are at romance, before concluding: 'British people don't seem to ask each other out.'

Where did we get the reputation as such notoriously bad seducers of women? The British male has always had his fair share of bad press in the seduction stakes and we seemingly need all the help we can get, which is why I was motivated to write *Right Woman, Right Now*. Clearly there is something peculiarly British that is truly beyond foreign visitors, especially women; this lack of understanding, compounded with their inability to really *hear* what we're saying, fuels the discrepancy between what is intended and what happens.

Our penchant for irony and understatement is something way beyond most other nationalities' understanding. Foreign women have never understood the subtlety of the British male, although now is the time to finally leave that quaint and traditional British gent behind and move on. The days of the tweed jacket, drophead MG, pipe and handlebar moustache ended about three decades ago, and it's time for the same seismic change that has happened to women over the past three decades. It's time that he became a little more boisterous and visibly assertive.

So for those who are lacking in a little confidence or technique, this book will help you overcome those first stumbling steps with hundreds of ideas and the wisdom of those men who are comfortable with women and find seducing them easier than the average male.

Right Woman, Right Now will give you the confidence, insider knowledge and short cuts you need to convert desire into tangible action and turn sexual opportunity into sexual reality. It offers a realistic game plan to understanding, approaching, engaging and seducing the modern woman.

1
You, the brand

Before we get on to the serious business of meeting and seducing women, let's start at the very beginning – with you. So you're not too tall, couldn't be mistaken for Colin Farrell (even on a dark night) and haven't got an Audi TT purring in the driveway. Or you're the opposite: very tall, too tall in fact, and your stomach is heading south faster than a plane load of drunken 18–30 holidaymakers. You know what? It matters, but not that much.

You've probably been pinballing from one situation to another, hoping to meet women and connect with them in a random haphazard way like atoms colliding – which can only lead to a high failure rate. All right, you've experienced some success but you know you could and should be doing infinitely better. Invariably you're getting rejected or meeting the wrong woman. If you really want to succeed with women it's like everything else, you need a game plan.

You need to start thinking of yourself as a brand and start streamlining your presentation. You have to be infinitely marketable to the opposite sex because there's a lot of competition out there and that competition is getting more intense and more proactive every day. You are a brand, a product, and the trick is creating demand – or rather, desire – for yourself.

When a company launches any product onto the market, whether it's a new drink, a new service or a new car, they go through a rigorous process of marketing from the initial research and development, production, through defining the market, distribution, point of sale, and on to customer feedback and refining the product.

You have to do the same and rethink your female strategy because the chances are that you are nowhere near reaching your true potential with women. In fact, you're selling yourself short. Without a game plan and without knowing your true target market you are not performing at your optimum, wasting valuable time, losing impact and, more importantly, losing market share; and I'm sure market share is one thing you want a bigger slice of.

Who are you and what are your brand values?

Why should a woman want to go out with you? Be honest with yourself – if you were a woman of some standing, why would you want to go out with you? What have you got to offer her that she would want? What qualities do you possess (or can at least acquire) that will appeal to your right woman and extend to an even wider audience? What is your brand promise? Strength? Integrity? Wisdom? Power?

What is your unique selling proposition?

Basically, what is it that you have got to offer over everybody else (i.e. other men, your competitors)? The trick is to make the best of the good marketable qualities you've got. But what is it you've got – dashing good looks, personality, style, an athletic build, an eye for fashion, the gift of the gab, money, power, intelligence, a way with animals or small children, the fact that you like women, a rock-hard set of abs or a huge penis? What, none of those? You must have something that is interesting, that you can market to women. Maybe you're as ugly as sin but you're a good listener. The solution? Get women talking about themselves and really listen.

Most men have at least one attribute that is attractive and endearing – work on refining that but also recognise what your weak points are and work on strengthening those too. Your average guy will have something they get extremely right and another thing that is so off-the-chart it actively works against them and sabotages any initial interest. For instance, you might have something attractive that enables a smooth connection, i.e. good looks, but then it all falls apart due to lack of delivery, because your verbal or physical skills don't match your first impression. Once you know where you are weak you can work on improving it. It's like golf – maybe you're driving is fantastic but your short game needs practice. So practise.

More appropriately, who is your target market?

You've probably spent your entire life to date hitting on every kind of woman you find even remotely attractive, i.e. anything with a decent set of breasts and legs – young, old, blonde, brunette, hippy, yuppie – without ever stopping to consider which type of woman really finds you attractive. And then you wonder why your strike rate is so poor?

You need to know where you stand in the pecking order of natural selection because natural selection is brutal, and you need to be honest with yourself about your expectations. Think about that for a moment – do your expectations match your physical appearance, financial standing, geographical location and social circumstances? If you're a hospital porter at Middlesex General Hospital and you refuse to go out with anyone less than Britney Spears, then you are deluding yourself and are destined for a non-existent love life and a lifetime of disappointment. Get real. It helps if you know who might fancy you.

How to find your attraction bracket

You need to find out what type of woman you appeal to and why you appeal to them. The object of this exercise is to find out which type of woman finds you attractive (and there will be many within a set range) and then seek out and present yourself to those women. Forget the rest for the time being. Of course, you will always score with various women who lie outside your 'attraction bracket' due to special circumstances – alcohol, the holiday fling, the chance meeting, the international conference, the surprise nymphomaniac – but by and large you should be able to narrow the field down to that 20 per cent of women where you will find 80 per cent of your success.

How to find out

You literally need to test the water by asking out real girls, which isn't a bad idea since it gets you into the swing of

things and gives you immediate practice. Ask out a range
of women – old, young, trendy, frumpy, everyone from that
old bag in Accounts to that gorgeous air stewardess who
lives in the flat two staircases across from you. Somewhere
in between you will find your range. You will be surprised
at their reaction.

Ask girlfriends
Find out what they honestly think of you and what they consider to be your good and bad points, taking in all aspects of
your presentation, from looks to style, speech and delivery.

Agency confirmation
There are agencies, particularly in Los Angeles and New York,
that will do this for you but I wouldn't recommend them as
they are seriously expensive and will add little to what you can
do for yourself.

History so far
What is your up-to-the-minute dating history? Which kind of
girls have you been successful with, and what approach did
you use to get them to go out with you? Of course, a snog and
grope behind the bicycle shed 15 years ago may not seem
important but it is all part of your dating history profile.
Remember that insane redhead who used to fancy you like
crazy and chased you halfway around the country? Why did
she fancy you? What aspect of your looks or personality drove
her crazy with lust and desire? What buttons did you press to
excite her?

Strangers
This is a great test of your personal character and is good
harmless fun if you pick the right woman. Go up to a strange

girl in a social situation and ask her if you can pick her brains for a minute. Say something along the lines of 'I'm changing my approach to women and I'd appreciate it if you wouldn't mind giving me a quick, honest, snapshot evaluation of your first impression of me. Given that I don't know you from a bar of soap.' No strings attached. If she's up for it she might give you ten minutes of solid advice. If she's even remotely positive and then asks, 'And what is your honest snapshot evaluation of me?' don't waste the opportunity. Say: 'I think you're completely gorgeous and would kill my granny to kiss you, right now.'

Rise above the competition

There are many mistakes most men make and if you can at least be aware of those and try and eradicate them from your personal repertoire, then you will stay ahead of the game. Most men:

- **Feel uncomfortable around women**, especially those they are particularly attracted to. It's a strange fact that when we're not so keen on a woman we can drive her mental with desire because we're confident, funny, relaxed, ourselves ... but when we're across a table from a woman we are insanely attracted to, whatever our age, our tongues get sticky, our palms sweaty, we forget the English language and any kind of social decorum.

- **Don't make the minimum required effort** women deem necessary to win their affections. Women love making men jump through hoops. How much do you care, how much do you love me? Will you pick up the dry cleaning on the way home? And they have a somewhat twisted gauge of how well we're doing.

- **Constantly sabotage their own efforts by reverting to 'typical male behaviour'.** So you get the girl and promise her a romantic night in with a candle-lit dinner, fine wine and all the trimmings. You've even changed the bed linen. You've been speaking about it for a week and she's so psyched up and ready to go she's almost slicing off her chair. Then, at the last minute, you stuff it up by remembering – at this eleventh hour – that you promised Dave you would fill in for him in the local five-a-side tournament. Bad move. This is real men-behaving-badly territory and will set your credibility back about five years. You've got to grow out of this.

- **Most men look like tramps 75 per cent of the time.** Worse, they are blissfully unaware that there is anything remotely wrong. If you're Brad Pitt and look fantastic even in mechanic's overalls, then fine, skip this paragraph. I'm assuming you're not, in which case do this – first look at yourself critically in the mirror. Let's do a quick five-point head-to-toe check:

  1. When did you last have a haircut? I don't mean that Italian barber you first went to with your dad when you were six. I mean a proper hairstylist, i.e. something that costs infinitely more than five quid and doesn't have sticky copies of *Fiesta* and *Escort* on the spare seat. Book an appointment now.

  2. Facial hair? Are you in or out? Are you seriously trying to grow something that replicates a beard or moustache, or is that fuzz just pure laziness? Any growth older than three days is not a fashionable 'shadow'.

  3. Don't you think you should throw that ratty old sweater away? Cable-knits are not fashionable.

Especially those that make you look like Starsky. That was the 1980s. Get with the programme.

4. When was the last time you cleaned or cut your nails? Would you like those grubby mangled tentacles all over your body, gliding in and out of your private nooks and crannies?

5. Do you change your underpants and socks frequently? If you're still smelling yesterday's smalls to see if they could last another day, you are in big trouble. (Check out the grooming rundown below).

- **Most men don't understand women.** You can argue that no man will ever fully understand women – men are from Mars, women are from Venus and all that – which is fair enough, but given the enormous female revolution that has taken place since *Cosmopolitan* first arrived in the UK in 1972 you surely can't have missed some of the propaganda that's been bandied about. You must have been exposed to and absorbed some of the trends and patterns of women's thinking and behaviour. You need to keep up to speed on where women are at and what their current issues are. Buy a couple of copies of *Cosmopolitan*, *Marie Claire*, *Red*, etc. and you will get a crash course in modern women's thinking.

- **Most men don't have any women friends.** This is a bad sign. It sends out a message that you don't like women or don't value them as people. You're missing a big trick here because women friends give you valuable insight into how women think and they tend to lead to other women. An introduction from a woman friend carries a lot more weight than a cold call.

- **Most men think women will come to them, eventually, if they are patient.** There's a group of men out there who really believe that Angelina Jolie is going to burst through the door of their Doncaster semi-detached demanding kinky sex if they wait long enough. Dream on, pal, this is never (repeat, never) going to happen. These men are seriously in denial. These are the same guys who arrange their bottles of Brut and Old Spice like trophies on top of their wardrobe. I cannot stress this often enough: meeting women is hard work and you have to put out. Women like men who make an effort.

Presentation skills – the art of good grooming

Generally the better you look the more confident you feel and the better the response from women. Packaging is *almost* everything. These days men are taking infinitely greater care of themselves than they did even five years ago, which women appreciate. It's a self-fulfilling prophecy. Being clean and looking healthy and fresh is something you can do very inexpensively, yet guys continue to go out hunting for women or turning up for dates in crap clothes looking, and smelling, like sweaty slobs and then wonder where the evening went so wrong. If you look like you don't care – especially when she's just spent an hour and a half getting ready – then she'll think you don't care, and she'll stop caring pretty fast.

Dress your age
Try and avoid dressing too young, or too old. A 23-year-old looks as stupid in a tweed jacket and Turnbull & Asser shirt, cable corduroys and Church brogues, as does a 45-year-old in silver platform trainers and a yellow Nike shell suit.

There is no shortage of expert, up-to-the-minute advice from the pages of at least ten monthly men's magazines and, again, the choice available to the average male is incredibly wide, the styling very versatile and good quality fashion is available across all income brackets. If you still look stupid in what you wear that's because you *are* stupid, because you can't be bothered to do a spot of research and the shopping that goes with it; not because there is nothing suitable on the market.

Check out magazines like *GQ, FHM, Esquire, Arena* and *Men's Health* – they practically do all the work for you, matching the right clothes with your body shape, age and personality. All right, some of the gear might be slightly pricey, or the male models might look a fraction dodgy, but the ideas are there for you to interpret. If you want to stand out and be ahead of the pack you need to work at it. Because other men are doing just that and even ordinary-looking guys are working on improving their chances by creating a better image that adds style and class, and boosts their confidence. Don't get left behind because of Neanderthal thinking. Get with the programme.

Good hair day

It's very easy to get stuck in a time warp and stay there, with your Rod Stewart feather-cut you've had since 'Maggie May' was first a hit. Look around you – hairstyles have moved on and change on a daily basis as embraced by each era's icon: Kevin Keegan's long locks, Gazza's blond Caesar cut, David Beckham's Alice-band fluff. The trick here though is to avoid the fad itself and find a cut that takes elements of the fad and is fashionable, but that suits the shape of your face and your lifestyle. For instance, if you go to the gym and shower a lot, go very short. Find a good stylist and go to the same one again and again and update your look every six months. Always bear in mind the three golden rules:

1. Never ever put your hair in a ponytail (even if you're a music biz exec or a film producer).

2. Never ever comb one long strand of hair over a bald patch, i.e. the dreaded comb-over.*

3. As you get older your hair should get shorter.

> **TIP:** *Bald heads always look better when tanned.*

Sound bodywork

You owe it to yourself to keep in reasonable shape, just 20 minutes of vigorous exercise a day will add ten years to your life, but apart from the obvious selfish health benefits, women do appreciate a hard body and tight bum if they can get their hands on one, and they prefer to be wrapped inside strong, not weedy, arms. Although don't overdo it – if you start looking like Arnold Schwarzenegger, you've gone way too far. Apart from looking like a shapely sack of potatoes, know that the bigger the muscles get the smaller the penis gets, so if you want to continue wearing extra-large underpants stay on the sensible side of muscle definition.

The aim here is to attain the classic V-shape, with big shoulders, toned arms, small waist and flat stomach to give the illusion of size and height. For some this is a laughable aspiration having spent a lifetime at the tuck shop, but for most guys, a

---

* Bald guys should take heart from the fact that bald is presently very 'in' and even young guys with forests of hair have actually been getting their heads shaved to look bald. So don't panic, although it's a good idea to try and keep some sort of even skin tone on the dome.

little running and light weight-work at the gym, or at home, can tighten up your body no end. Grab a couple of issues of *Men's Health* or *Men's Fitness* and you'll pick up a few routines. A good three-mile run two or three times a week should keep your tummy trim. Although, quite honestly, I'd forget about the classic six-pack – if you can't see your abs at the moment you're never going to see them without a monumental amount of harsh nutritional discipline and regular hard physical work. Rather work towards a trim, toned, fit body than obsess about your abs. If you can still see your flaccid penis when standing, you're winning. The other thing about an over-gymed body is that women can get extremely jealous – not necessarily of your physical anatomy but more about the time you spend achieving it. As a rough gauge, if you spend more time in front of the mirror primping and preening than she does, then you've got a mutiny on your hands.

Flesh tones

Some Brits have blotchy, fair skin at the best of times (I blame the Vikings), but a few sessions at the local beauty salon in the Tan Can or on a sunbed, or an early holiday if you can afford it, will even out your skin tones and give you a healthy glow. The range of men's cleansing products available has exploded since Clinique first put their ladies cleanser in a chunky bottle and called it Scuffing Lotion for men, about 15 years ago. Every upmarket fragrance brand now has a men's range of toiletries, so there's no excuse for body odours and unsightly skin complaints. If you're blinded by cosmetic science, pick one of the better-looking girls on the cosmetic counter of your local department store and cry for help. She'll love it. There are any number of moisturisers, toners and cleansers in nice, male-friendly, chunky packaging from Clinique to Aramis, etc. so there's no excuse, and it is no longer considered girlie to look after your skin. A clear fresh complexion is infinitely more kissable than a dry, blotchy, pizza face.

Facial eruptions

Don't mess around with adult spots, i.e. if you're over 18 and still get that embarrassing yellow-headed zit on the end of your nose or chin at crucial moments, forget all those washes and creams and go straight to see a dermatologist. I always used to suffer from that one greasy blot on my facial landscape until this skin specialist gave me a short course of Cyclamine tablets. Since then, zit free.

Forward thinking

Forget your frontal probe, think with your frontal lobe. That thing between your ears is the sexiest organ in the world so let's start to think with that, shall we? It's where sex begins and ends so don't discount what it's telling you. Your first instinct is usually not far off the mark so if your brain says, 'This girl is far too young' or 'She's a psycho', back off. If it says, 'Mm, that's tasty, you're in there' or 'Hurry up, she's gagging for it', move on it.

Block and tackle

Keep your penis clean and in good working order. Make sure it's pink and shiny and in peak condition. There's a tendency for the penis to collect smegma (i.e. cheese) under the foreskin (if you've got one) and smell if not washed properly, which is not a very nice surprise for any woman to find, and very disappointing for you if you were hoping for some oral action. Always allow time for a shower between work and play. Otherwise, don't be shocked when she stops kissing you tenderly, sits bolt upright and says, 'Let's watch some telly.'

Sports guys might want to dust their balls regularly with talc to stop that jockey rash, and while you're at it you might want to check your nuts for any irregularities, i.e. hard lumps on the testicle itself. Surprisingly, testicular cancer kills more men than breast cancer kills women, so if anything feels the slightest bit odd see the guy with the stethoscope.

Whatever your current 'marital' status, masturbate at least once a day. Apart from the obvious private enjoyment, it will keep the hormones alert and used to the idea of sex, clean your tubes and keep the sperm factory flowing. Once you know it's in good working order, leave it alone until you need it, i.e. stop touching it, to see if it's still there. It isn't going anywhere without you. And stop thinking with it!

Mouthing off

The mouth is probably your most crucial piece of anatomy. You're going to need it for talking, kissing and flashing that irresistible smile. Test your breath often; when you're dehydrated you tend to get a horrendous stale aroma, which is not attractive, so keep your fluid intake high. Not many people will tell you that your breath stinks – they just find an excuse to leave the room, fast. Rely on a good mate or girl 'friend' instead.

> **TIP:** *Don't forget to brush the tongue as well as the teeth. Your lips should be moist and shiny – not dry and scaly – and cold-sore free. Buy some lip balm and keep them in good condition.*

Say 'cheese'

We Brits have the worst dental reputation in the world. Think David Bowie and The Pogues and you get the idea. Medical researchers are now predicting that we are all going to live to be 100, which means we are going to outlive our teeth (and pensions) unless we start looking after them. Cosmetic dentistry is prohibitively expensive and painful, but well worth it if you're not blessed with a good set of goobers or an unfortunate overbite. Once it's done, it's done and your self-esteem will explode.

The other trick is to whiten the ones you've got which involves a private process of bleaching that is relatively inexpensive, although a pain in the ass. There's no substitute for brushing and flossing your teeth and gums properly, and experts recommend a Braun electric toothbrush – five seconds on each tooth twice a day. Once the gums get diseased, it's all over. The odd missing tooth from a noble rugby battle adds a certain cavalier warrior air, but a set of false teeth in a glass of Steradent on the bedside table is about as big a passion-killer as you can get.

Hands down

You'll need them for touching, caressing and massaging, so they really need to be clean and in good condition. Keep your nails short and brush them often – yet another excuse to talk to Susan at the beauty clinic – and try to remember to rub some moisturising cream in, especially if you're a rough, tough hombre with a manual job like lumberjacking. You don't want your hard skin lacerating her soft tissue.

Play footsie for me

So she invites you to test out her fresh Irish linen and you dive into her bed with grubby, dirty feet covered in calluses. Big mistake. You can get rid of athlete's foot and planters' warts and keep them under control with over-the-counter remedies, however, if you need to get rid of that stubborn wart or verruca, go and get it zapped at the chiropodist. One hit of liquid nitrogen and a week later it drops off. Get a pedicure every three months and you will get rid of that build-up of hard skin that might otherwise ladder a woman's tights when you're running your foot up her leg. There's no excuse for having bad feet.

The eyes have it

Eyes are the windows of the soul and this is what your woman is going to be spending a lot of time concentrating on, so it helps if they are sparkling and fresh, and not tired and blood-shot with huge bags under them. A good night's sleep isn't a bad idea – you don't want to turn up for a hot date looking like a burnt-out bloodhound – and slip yourself a couple of hits of vitamins B and C and your eyes will shine. Failing that ask your pharmacist for an over-the-counter eye drop that will whiten the eyes in a hurry.

NOTE: *If you're one of those guys with thick, telephone-cable, Dennis Healey eyebrows ask your hairdresser to give them a trim when she does your hair.*

Chariots of fire – car sense

Whatever is claimed to the contrary, it's a fact that women do gravitate towards men with a halfway decent motor. A clapped-out VW Beetle may be fun and exciting when you're a teenager and it's your first car, but you only have to break down once at an inopportune moment and the object of your desire will quickly move on to a more reliable model, and driver.

As you move up the ladder of quality women, you will find them increasingly picky about the chariot you arrive in to whisk them away, which is also a measure of the occasion. Turn up in a fourth-hand 1980s Honda rust-bucket to take her to her office open night where she needs to impress her colleagues, and you are toast.

> **TIP:** *If you do have a crap car or no car, organise to hire a decent one for that special evening, when she needs to show off. You'll pick up major brownie points. If you can't drive, learn fast or get a chauffeur.*

You can also overdo it by driving something that is so far out it becomes kitsch and embarrassing, or a parody of itself. Everyone hates a show-off so if you arrive in a bright orange Lamborghini Countach burning rubber, the chances are a) she won't recognise what car it is anyway, which defeats the object, and b) it would be too far over the top for her. You don't have to be so obviously clichéd and ostentatious. Even if you've got a stack of cash the better option is to choose something sexy and smooth that doesn't stick out like a sore thumb.

> **TIP:** *Resist the temptation to spend all your Sundays doing up some wreck. These days, with improved technology, long warranties and motor plans, it's far more economical to buy a nearly new car than throw money at an old banger in the vain hope of saving a couple of hundred quid. The time you spend under the bonnet could be better spent chasing your right woman and I promise you, by the time you've finished doing up the old banger, you'll probably have spent more money than buying a new car.*

Drive a man's car

This is a very important yet often overlooked concept. The car market is subliminally split up into girls' cars and boys' cars,

straight cars and gay cars, young cars and old cars, so whatever you do don't be perceived to be driving a girl's car, e.g. a
Fiat Uno, or VW Polo; or a gay car, e.g. a Suzuki Jeep or the
new Beetle. Also, get a car that matches your size and age. If
you're, let's say, slightly chubby or seriously tall, don't drive a
Mini Cooper S. If you've just turned 18 you'll look daft in a
Mercedes SL500, or a 7-series BMW; equally, a distinguished
55-year-old looks stupid in a purple Vauxhall Corsa, even with
go-faster stripes. I'm sure you get the idea.

Convertible fun

Driving a convertible, when the weather permits, is a very fun
and full-on social experience as well as a powerful babe
magnet. Women wind down their windows and talk to you
and people shout at you from vans and buses. Pedestrians
throw comments at you from the pavement and everywhere
you go there's a complete carnival atmosphere that is something you never experience in a normal saloon.

If you're stuck at a slow red light in front of, behind or adja-
cent to a hot babe and you switch down the automatic top on
a SAAB, BMW or a Mercedes, watch her drool as the roof goes
down and magically disappears. Smile and wave and shout
across to her.

Women really do go all gooey for convertibles. Be warned,
though, the perception is better than the reality. Once her hair
starts getting whipped across her face in the jet stream and it
gets a bit chilly, it won't be long before she says, 'Would you
mind if we put the roof back on?'

> **TIP:** *When taking a girl for a drive in a convertible, always
> ask her to bring a headscarf. Longish hair will sting her eyes
> and she'll quickly get very miserable. And always carry some*

factor 30 suntan lotion in the glove compartment and insist (repeat, insist) that she use it. One seemingly quick spin from London to Brighton on a hot summer's day and by 3 p.m. she'll look like lobster thermidor; which does not go down well. Equally, if it's chilly, be sensitive to her needs – you might well be tucked up in a sheepskin coat but if she's only wearing a thin cocktail dress, ask her if she's warm enough before she turns blue.

NOTE: *When you get home don't forget to put the roof up before you move inside with the babe for a heavy session. You don't want to wake up the next morning with a car full of rainwater.*

What's your marketing strategy?

This will change almost on a daily basis as your mood and your state of mind dictate the rules of your particular game, and the opportunities presented seal your fate. Where you look for them and what you do with them when you've found them is a measure of what type of result you are looking for. It will depend on what type of woman or relationship you're looking for – a one-night stand, a long-term relationship, marriage, an affair. Don't be afraid of being flexible. You might set out to find a blonde with magnificent breasts who is devoted to a single life of unashamed hedonism. But if, along the way, you fall madly in love with a flat-chested brunette with two children, don't fight it. Go with the flow.

2
Acquiring the right attitude

Why do all the dorks always get the babes?
Because dorks make a bigger effort. So who's the dork now?

Confidence counts

Confidence is that intangible X-factor that a man exudes when he feels comfortable and in charge of any given situation. If you've got it you feel capable of almost anything. A lack of confidence leads to uncertainty and indecisiveness – that dithering smog – and smacks of fear and low esteem, two qualities that women find grossly unattractive.

Avoiding the Valley of the Wimps

We've all been there. Every man jack one of us. It's that horrible place where you turn into a yellow-livered, custard-spined, wet blanket; when your courage and confidence evaporate before your very eyes. That horrendous feeling when you know you've let that one *right woman* go that you should have worked harder for and you're now a nonsense of 'if only'. It may have just been a question of talking to her at the bar, picking up a phone and dialling her number or effecting a 'coincidental chance meeting', but for whatever reason you bottled out. And now you feel disappointed in yourself as you witness her disappearance from your radar, often with another man. The 'valley' is a place to avoid at all costs.

How many times have you been in that situation where you see some hot babe and she's together with what you consider to be some completely unsuitable dork? You stop and take a double take and wonder, 'Why do all the dorks always get the babes?' The answer is simple: because dorks make a bigger effort. So who's the dork now? You'd better get your skates on, before the passion police knock on your door to give you your virginity back. Maybe you've never had a proper girlfriend and feel uncomfortable around women. Maybe you recently found your wife of fifteen years in bed with the next-door neighbour and are feeling slightly bruised and nervous of the dating jungle. Maybe you're just pumped full of testosterone with nobody to share it with.

Whatever the reason you haven't got a girlfriend, the time has come to get one – the *right one*.

Regaining your confidence

If you haven't had a girlfriend for a while, for whatever reason, then you've probably experienced a certain loss of confidence, stopped making an effort or fallen into that terrible habit of pretending that you don't really want or need one – consoling yourself, instead, with the comfort of a late-night movie or last week's footy highlights.

Yet every time that drop-dead babe from the bookshop zips past in her GTi cabriolet, hair blowing in the slipstream, her tight crop top accentuating perky breasts, you get a sudden twinge in your loins. Especially when you watch her getting out of the car, long, shapely caramel legs first. You're sure she must have a regular boyfriend in tow – she probably has, but why can't that boyfriend be you?

If it's been a while then you can quietly despair whether or not you'll ever get another girlfriend in your life and resign yourself to the comfort of a six-pack of beer and a takeaway curry in front of the cricket. The longer you leave it the harder it is to get back into the swing of things, and realise that in this modern, fast-paced world, the rules and etiquette of dating are changing pretty much as we speak. Relax. Things aren't *that* bad – you just need to get back in the driving seat. Here's how.

First, stop making excuses

Anyone can be passive. Anyone can be lazy and uninspired, unimaginative and unadventurous, and think of a thousand excuses why they're not out there fighting for their rightful position, next to their right woman. It's safe and cosy; but extremely boring. Just order a pizza, grab a video, water the plants and close your eyes to the opportunity that is out there; convincing yourself that you're having a great time. But you know, and I know, that you'd much rather be spending a night full of passion and waking up next to some hot woman. Apart from anything else, it's embarrassing. You get to work on

Monday and when they ask did you have a great weekend, everyone else seems to have been rutting like stags, and what did you do? You went to a movie, alone. In the afternoon so that nobody would see you. You might even invent some fantasy woman that you're involved with so that your pals don't think you're an utterly sad basket case.

Remember, while you're not chatting up your right woman, somebody else is. It takes courage to grab your coat, slap on a bit of Eau Sauvage, get out there and mingle. But listen, there isn't much time. You've got another 40 good years if you're lucky and you could be zapped in a suicide bombing tomorrow. At the risk of sounding too macabre, think 9/11 (and I don't mean the Porsche). It's quite telling that in the months following 9/11 the whole of New York City went on a shagging spree of note. Tomorrow you die, so make love now while you've got the chance. Lecture over. So get to it. Get a little bit of action in your life. Get it tonight.

Excuse No. 1: But there aren't any women

Look, don't give me that 'I never seem to meet any women' argument, or 'I never seem to see any women I like'. You are either blind or deceiving yourself. The country is teeming with brilliant women of every conceivable type, colour, creed, and degree of beauty and sexiness. There are about four straight women to every straight guy. There are women everywhere. Don't believe me? First, do this:

Observation therapy

Go to your nearest decent shopping centre in the middle of a Saturday morning. Find yourself a good observation spot at the best, trendy coffee bar, order a cappuccino and just observe. If you're a little on the shy side, take a newspaper as a prop and pretend you're reading it.

And what do you see before your very eyes? That's right, women: old ones, young ones, tall ones, small ones, fat ones, thin ones; redheads, blondes, brunettes and the odd breathtaking uber-babe of gorgeous proportions. Given the statistics, if you're somewhere like Brent Cross, then you will probably have seen ten women flash by who would be the perfect match for you as a life partner.

Next, try this: observe how many of these women are alone and how many of these women are with men. Concentrate for a moment on those with a man and check out the calibre of these men. You will swiftly deduce that many a gorgeous-looking babe is hanging on to the arms of a complete social jerk who is far less handsome, witty, athletic, sophisticated, caring and charming than your good self. They certainly don't deserve to be putting their hands on her breasts, kissing her all over and making love to such a goddess. But they are. And you're not.

Conclusion: Yes there are zillions of terrific women about and half of those are going out with men who aren't even remotely as eligible as you are.

Excuse No. 2: But they're never going to fancy me

It's easy to get carried away with life's stereotypes, thinking that all women go for tall, dark and handsome, or healthy and wealthy, and worry that you will never make the grade. Thing is, yes, just like everyone else, women have a dream date like you do – theirs is probably Brad Pitt or Colin Firth; yours probably lies somewhere between Jordan and Charlize Theron – but the reality is, we all need to connect with someone in tangible, not virtual, reality. It's in our genes, and if we're not in a position to get inside the jeans of our dreams, we generally opt for somebody more down to earth; which is why 99.9

per cent of the women on the planet who haven't got their personal Brad Pitt in tow would die to choose you.

Second, stop taking women so seriously, and literally

Over the past thirty years, with the onset and maturing of feminism through its many stages from hostile to less so to positively lethargic, man's confidence, particularly his sexual confidence, has been eroded to the point of obsolescence. His sperm count and fertility are diminishing, his potency withering – half the male population appear to be on Viagra or erection-inducing drugs or injections – or are trying to surgically enhance their penises. We are, seemingly, in bad shape.

Women have been hostile and bullying, telling men to be more like a woman and encouraging men to cry more and get in touch with their feelings. In bed, women have been increasingly demanding as their confidence has risen; and woe betide any man who orgasms before they do, or worse, who can't get it up. Then there are the false cries of rape and sexual harassment that have scattered the press, leaving broken men littering the pavement. Articles in *Time* and myriad women's magazines have posed the question: Are Men Obsolete?

Confusion reigns supreme

All this female empowerment and consequent male downsizing have conspired to render the average man dazed and confused and seemingly paralysed with fear. It's hardly surprising that men are feeling slightly bruised and abused, and it's a miracle any man can find the courage to be on the same planet as a woman, never mind approach her for a date.

Confusion reigns supreme and the mixed messages that

women are still giving off can be frustrating if you don't read between the lines. The average man still doesn't know whether or not to open a door, or leave it closed. If he were to see a woman with a flat tyre should he drive on or stop to help and risk getting his head bitten off with a barrage of insults? 'I'm very capable of changing it myself.'

> **TIP:** *Just be polite. When it comes to door opening, I'd hold the door open for a stranger whether it is male or female, young or old, simply out of politeness.*

Women have changed their minds every five minutes: first they wanted the new man, that elusive, sensitive new-age guy; then they decided that he was far too soft and girlie and collectively agreed that, actually, they wouldn't mind if he was a bit of a bastard, i.e. a strong man and a bit of a rebel, but not abusive to women.

Symbolic of all this mind-changing is the Paula Cole song 'Where have all the cowboys gone?' lamenting the passage of the real man, the Marlboro man if you like. Where have all the cowboys gone? They're alive and kicking and living in Lewisham, but presently their boots and spurs need polishing and they're feeling a little subdued.

The good news

You can swallow the media hype and propaganda about sisters-under-the-skin and man's obsolescence, but that's all it is – hype. Rest assured, the average woman still craves male company and is desperate to find a real soulmate to have fun with, have great conversation and sex with, settle down with and give her a cuddle in front of a weepy or scary movie.

There's no sperm bank on the planet that can do all that. Test tubes do not get spiders out of the bath. She's looking for you as hard as you are looking for her.

STRATEGY SESSION:
12 STEPS TO BABE HEAVEN

1. Push yourself

We all make self-imposed rules and barriers for ourselves that limit our vision and potential. We generally play safe in most areas of our lives and keep doing what we know works rather than risk anything (especially rejection) by experimenting. With women it's easier to find a comfort zone and nestle into that for the rest of your life rather than seek new challenges, but really there is so much going on outside of your comfort zone. You need to push yourself. The ego is the easiest thing to risk since it doesn't cost you anything apart from time and a temporarily bruised spirit, but that doesn't last long. You need to be open to new thinking and explore new avenues of opportunity. Stop being so passive and waiting for things to happen – you must be the one to make things happen. You need to be the driver, the innovator, the leader. Women respect that.

2. Practice makes perfect

Remember how in the playground you and your mates used to practise keepy-uppy or played with a football for hours on end? Seducing a woman is no different. The more you do it the better you get. Accept that you will fail some of the time. Of course you're going to make a fool of yourself along the way. So what? The trick is to have the confidence to go out and do it and make the effort. The more you do it, the easier it gets and the better you get at it. At first what you come up with when you approach a woman may be utter drivel. Crass, ridiculous crap you can't believe trips off your tongue, combined with the body language of a swirling dervish. But after a little practice you'll find out what works for you and you'll see success. You'll be alarmed at how proficient you will become and the situations you will find yourself in.

3. Be addictive

A friend of mine is short but hasn't got a complex about it, he's not great looking but doesn't really worry about it and he always has a smart woman on his arm. What he is though, above all else, is addictive and don't underestimate the potency of this one quality. He is habit forming. Why? At first women look at him and think, *no way*. But because he doesn't appear to be a contender they lower their guard and allow him to enter their world. They start to feel very comfortable around him. Pretty quickly they find that not only are they getting on well with him, they are actually enjoying his company. Suddenly they are really liking him – a lot – and wanting to be with him all the time. He's funny, he's smart, he dresses well, he's attentive, he notices their style, he's generous and he altogether makes women feel fabulous. And he's comfortable with himself. He chips away at them and gets right under their skin. And they just keep coming back for more. They get addicted and need their fix of him on a regular basis. It bears notice.

4. Don't give up

You've got to be persistent and not take the first refusal from a woman as set in stone. You've got to grab any opportunity and stick with it like a stubborn Jack Russell on a stranger's trouser leg. Unfortunately we men tend to give up far too easily – one 'thanks, but no thanks' or one withering look and a man will back off, skulk away and sulk in the corner for weeks. Don't. Look, if a woman has said 'no' a thousand times and she's taken out a court order against you being within a 150-mile exclusion zone of her, then you can swiftly deduce that she's not the slightest bit interested. Move on. But in a normal situation, even if you do get an initial rejection, try and leave the issue 'open' or on the table' like a long-running negotiation rather than a fait accompli. Let her know that you will be back and that you are still very interested despite her momentary reticence (and obvious lapse of clear thinking). Women change their minds about everything – often. It is a female prerogative and she might change her mind about you sooner than you think. Because circumstances change.

In the short term
Best example of this is a nightclub or party when circumstances and human dynamics change literally by the minute and by the amount of alcohol consumed. Personal standards can drop faster than the share price of Enron and Martha Stewart put together. You've probably seen this scenario played out many times before your very eyes, but have never actually analysed it.

The set-up. At the beginning of the evening, that hot blonde thinks that she's going to make it with the dashing guy in the Armani suit. Consequently, when you talk to her she's surly, cold and unfriendly. A few other guys have a bash, but meet the same fate. Shot down in flames over hostile territory.

But then, suddenly, the rules change. After a flirtatious interchange and a couple of dances with the hot blonde, Mr Armani suit is visibly unimpressed and moves in on the giggly redhead with the big tits and they disappear. Buzz! He's out of the game and the hot blonde is now exposed and vulnerable.

Suddenly the blonde is psychologically at a disadvantage. She feels slighted and her ego has been damaged – and this happened publicly, in full view of a group of people who are probably her friends. Not only that, the handful of not-too-shabby guys with potential who showed interest in her earlier have been cold-shouldered, so have lost interest and moved on.

Consequently she's in a tight spot. She's put all her eggs in one basket and the clumsy git in the Armani suit has trampled all over them. She needs to claw back respect and display tangible proof that she is indeed as attractive as she thinks she is to restore her rightful position in the pecking order. She now needs lashings of attention, fast.

Talk to her now and the chances are she certainly won't be surly and might actually be welcoming. In fact, I bet that if you walked over to her with a drink, right now, she'd be all over you like a rash. Go on.

In the long term

Like hot property, your right woman could suddenly come back on to the market after a prolonged period off it at *any* time. Seemingly secure, long relationships can come to an abrupt end for a variety of reasons, not least being one of the parties having been caught having an affair.

Couples often just grow out of each other too. As I write this, a girl 'friend' of mine has just dumped her boyfriend-cum-fiancé – and I thought it was a relationship cemented in heaven. They were engaged to be married and had spent a year living together, the wedding was booked, invitations printed and all the trimmings. You would have thought that she was off the mailing list for ever.

Not any more. She told me yesterday that it was all over, that she had moved out and they, as an item, were toast due to irre-concilable differences. What's interesting about long-term couples is that when the game is still on they are so consumed with each other that they tend to neglect their existing friendships. When the split happens they suddenly find that they have no real sup-port system. That's precisely what happened here.

So here's a highly desirable and attractive woman, slightly bruised but not bitter, back to square one: lonely and available. I wonder what went so horribly wrong. More appropriately, I won-der what she's doing tonight?

5. Persistence pays off

I was once squeezed in a packed lift at Belsize Park tube station
and this gorgeous girl in the furthest corner rolled her eyes and
flashed me a huge smile. I could tell through her eyes, even
between the heaving, sweaty crowd, that she was interested.
There was something going on. My knees were so weak that if I
hadn't been squeezed between two fatties, I would have fallen
over.

The doors flew open, the crowd spilled out and when the chaos
had abated, I looked for her everywhere —but she was gone. She'd
literally vanished into the ether. She must have slipped out of the
far side of the lift and disappeared through the other entrance. I
was gutted.

I couldn't get her out of my mind all weekend and decided that
I had to meet her. What to do? I couldn't rely on a chance meeting on the way to, or back, from work. Instead I spent a week
waiting patiently on the bench outside the tube station reading a
paper. I'd get there an hour before I had to set off for work and
returned an hour earlier from work and stayed an hour later, hoping she would arrive. After about the fourth day this was getting
slightly tedious and I had my doubts – I actually *lived* in Belsize
Park but what if she was just visiting a friend?

Then, on the fifth morning I saw her walking towards the tube.
My heart was pumping like a maniac, but I casually joined the
crocodile of passengers and moved closer and closer to her. When
we got on the train I could barely breathe but I elbowed a couple
of grannies out of the way and engineered that I squeezed in
next to her. There was that smile again.

'Hi, I haven't seen you for ages. How are you?' I said in the
most casual manner I could muster, as if we were old friends. She
was fantastic, very easy-going, and by the time we got to
Tottenham Court Road I had her telephone number, knew half
her life story and we had a date for the evening. Actually, 'date' is

probably too strong a word. It was nothing fancy – we met after work and went for fish and chips at the restaurant opposite the tube station before going back to my place. The start of a very enjoyable three-month romance.

Now if you think that's persistent, the CEO of Condé Nast UK, Nicholas Coleridge, tells a story of how he chased his 'right woman', now his wife, from London to India and back. He basically engineered that he 'bump into' his desired target while she was on holiday.

6. Make her feel special

This is not rocket science but it's something we men overlook. All women love to be made to feel special. The beauty of this is a) it doesn't cost anything (well, not much), and b) they love it and lap it up. But how do you make a woman feel special? Try these easy tactics:

- **Listen to her.** This is the easiest and cheapest thing, yet the most potent. All you have to do is listen, and I mean *really* listen, to what she is saying. Not that half-assed nodding and grunting that we men are so good at. Let her know that you have listened and heard, by repeating part of her sentence in your conversation.

- **Look at her.** Don't take your eyes off her for a minute. Don't even glance away. Sit at the table with her and glue your eyes to hers, riveted. I guarantee that she will never have had such attention lavished upon her.

- **Talk to her,** engage her and entertain her. If you know any snippet of hot gossip, share it with her.

- **Involve her.** To show you value her, ask her opinion on something personal to you whether it be the purchase of your new suit, or the design of the logo for your new business.

- **Share a secret with her.** Women love being told a secret whether it be a personal one or about somebody else. Whisper it in her ear and watch her giggle or begin that conspiratorial intimacy that women do so love.

- **Buy her a present.** You don't have to, but it is a nice touch, particularly if it has special meaning, such as a memento of your first date. It doesn't have to be expensive either; the trick is in the wrapping – in a nice box or with a bow and good quality paper.

7. Put her off

Sometimes you find yourself in a situation whereby a spot of reverse psychology goes a long way to realising your goal. Give a woman a reason why you can't possibly go out with her and she will invariably counter the argument and end up fighting your battle for you. She starts actively talking herself *into* going out with you.

'I'm far too old for you; you wouldn't understand me' intimidates her and challenges her to rise to the bait. Of course her effort to prove that she can handle you circumvents whether or not she feels you are attractive in the first place, which has become secondary to winning the argument.

You can shift the emphasis from her – as in 'you're too young to understand and handle me' – on to your own deficiency which will cause her to rise to your defence. For instance, if you say something like, 'Nah, you don't want to go out with me; everyone will think you're my daughter', or 'I couldn't possibly keep up with you, you walk too damn fast', she will counter it with a solution. Strange tactics but try it.

8. Learn to dance properly

Dancing really is a brutal public display of your physical dexterity, revealing your sense of fun and level of inhibition to all. The subliminal message women pick up is that if you can't dance, or you dance awkwardly, you'd be a complete disaster in bed. Women warm to men who can dance properly and the trick here is to make *them* look good on the dance floor. You must have witnessed that common scenario where some ugly stranger suddenly becomes the hit of the party because he knows a few slick dance steps and starts throwing babes around the dance floor like John Travolta. Suddenly the women go all gooey and are literally queuing up for a turn like five-year-olds at Disney World, as the non-dancing guys look down into their pints in subdued embarrassment.

So get some rhythm

White guys generally dance as if they are stepping on cockroaches, so if you do dance like a wooden puppet ask a girl 'friend' to give you some pointers before they start calling you Pinocchio. Better still spend a week or so at a local dance studio on the quiet (check Yellow Pages). First of all you'd probably meet at least one decent woman at the class and in half a dozen lessons you can learn all the classic moves (waltz, tango, foxtrot) while gaining the required sense of contemporary rhythm and physical confidence women find attractive.

> **TIP:** *Once you're dancing with a hot babe, don't destroy the moment by immediately trying to stick your knee up her crotch or animatedly pumping her ass in front of her friends.*

9. Don't forget to flirt

Flirting is one of the main ways you can convert a maybe into a certainty. Women are fantastic at flirting, they actively encourage it and really enjoy it, yet time and again we men fail to capitalise and take advantage of this fact. We tend to be more reserved and see everything in black or white – either you fancy me or you don't, let's cut to the chase and do something about it or move on. The inference being: I'm a busy man so don't waste my time if you're not interested.

Faced with such ultimatums is it any wonder that most women can't be bothered? They've invited you to play and you've spurned their invitation. Wrong move.

Converting a maybe into a certainty

Flirting inhabits that grey area between yes and no, and it is during flirting that you have the opportunity to convert a 'maybe' or a 'possible' into a 'certainty'. Flirting is communicating at a high level and while you still have the channels open, the situation is very alive and can go either way. You want the woman to come back at you and say, reading between the lines, I'm glad I stuck around. I didn't realise you were so smart, funny, attractive and compatible.'

Many men (and women) actually forget how to flirt and how important it is to the process of seduction. I've seen it a million times especially with divorced women who have probably spent the last 18 months fighting with their ex, and see flirting as hollow frippery; they've been out of the singles scene for a while and have literally forgotten the fun element of banter and verbal or physical teasing, and see it as an unnecessary, time-wasting hindrance to the dating process. Big mistake.

10. Learn to speak hocus-pocus

Women love talking about palmistry and astrology and other spiritual, fortune-teller types of quasi-sciences. The star sign conversation has been done to death yet remains perennially fascinating to some women (Scorpios are sexy and secretive; Aquarians are caring; Geminis are psychotic, schizophrenic bastards), but if you can pick up a few basics of either astrology or palmistry – i.e. the love line, the fate line and the crinkles in your skin that reveal how many children you're going to have – then you can keep a woman entertained and focused on you for hours while you actually hold her hand. And have others queuing up for a turn. The same applies to those other girlie 'sciences' like reiki, reflexology and aromatherapy. I'm not going to waste your valuable time here, but when you've got a minute, punch the keyword 'Reiki' or 'Palmistry' into your favourite search engine on the Internet and you could be an expert by the time you hit the bar tonight: 'Excuse me, can I see your hand? Wow, your life line's a mile long.' Don't overdo it though – leave the bandana and hoop earrings at home.

TIP: *Don't forget to litter your conversation with the odd compliment, e.g. 'Mm, nice nails' or 'Beautiful long fingers – you should have been a pianist.'*

11. Know that you can change her mind

You must have borne witness to the scenario where some woman in the office has been voicing her negative opinion of a guy: 'He's such an arrogant prick' or 'He thinks he's God's gift' and the rest. Then she suddenly meets him in a social situation or a one-on-one chance meeting and the next thing she's absolutely gushing: 'I was really wrong about him, he's actually quite charming.'

You have the power to change a woman's mind about you. You have the power to change her mind. All you need to do is find out what the stumbling block is – why does she think you're big-headed or pig-headed? Soften your approach; change your behaviour or speech pattern. Talk about her not you. Whatever was wrong, change – whatever it takes – even brutal honesty. Go back to see her and say, 'Look, I'm conscious of the fact that we got off on the wrong foot and I'd like it if we could start again. What do you say?' Most women will give you another chance.

12. Learn to cook

Think Naked Chef. If Jamie Oliver can woo the entire female population of the planet with his chicken breasts and homemade pesto, then you should be able to get one or two food-seeking females along to sample your chilli con carne. Women love men who can cook and ever since Michael Caine cooked a meal in The Ipcress File as Hollywood's first soft, sensitive super spy, men have been actively incorporating food into their seduction repertoire. If the best you can manage is a chip butty then it might be an idea to check out a few cookery courses, of which there are many. The beauty of this is that you get to interact with women at the course who will outnumber you by about ten to one.

The arsenal of the babe magnet

Men who are at ease, self-confident and successful with women generally display a range of male seduction skills that women are drawn to and which are not impossible to acquire if you are, sadly, lacking in some of them.

You need to be vigilant

You've got to keep your eyes peeled for when opportunities present themselves, because we men generally miss an awful lot. Look, some guys just never notice babes. Kate Moss, Scarlett Johannson and Keira Knightley could all walk into the bar stark naked, start lap dancing on your table and some guys would still keep blabbering on about their second putt on the tenth green at Elstree. Even those of us who think we never miss a trick need to be constantly on the lookout, radar on. If you fail to notice those subtle facial and bodily nuances – and remember, women think they're being dangerously obvious when they raise an eyebrow – then this could cost you an entertaining evening.

You need to have presence

This is the impact that you make when you enter a room and a measure of how much attention you can command in a group of people. It's a natural instinct for the 'herd' or the 'pack' to look around and check out a newcomer in a group situation, just to make sure the interloper isn't carrying a spear, or to check out whether or not he/she is a worthy mate. So try and capture as much of that initial natural attention as you can. Here, less is more. A slow, measured scan of the room (open expression) should throw up at least one interested party who locks your gaze, smiles or raises an eyebrow (let's hope it's not that guy in the pink shirt).

You need good presentation skills

You've got to look the part. This means dressing your age, not your shoe size, and dressing appropriately for any given situation or function; knowing the meaning of black tie, smart casual and casual smart as well as what clothes and accessories demonstrate your personal 'brand image' and maximise your personal impact. (See Presentation Skills, page 13)

You need to be patient

Rush it and you blow it. You can't just go up to a woman, blurt out some crass line and think she's going to take her clothes off and fall in love with you. Seduction is an art form as complicated as landing a trout. And you certainly don't yank a trout out of the water without a monumental amount of line being let out, and then slowly reeled in. Providing you're not in a rush (see Creating a sense of urgency, page 129) and you know where to find the same woman again, then take time to get your ducks in a row.

You need to have wit

If you can make a woman laugh, then you're halfway there, goes the thinking – and it's very true. Well, almost true. British women generally have a refined sense of humour. But this doesn't mean telling jokes. If you find yourself saying things like, 'You're going to love this one. It's really funny. There was this Irishman this Scotsman and ...' stop yourself. Wit is the clever use of words, ideas and mannerisms to produce a fun moment that others appreciate. The easiest way to engage humour is to start by laughing at yourself. This puts everyone at ease.

You need to have charm

This is knowing and using your manners without being a doormat; being able to compliment a woman without it sounding like you've been rehearsing it for two days. Knowing when your date feels uncomfortable in any situation and is ready to leave. Taking into consideration and anticipating her feelings.

You need to be generous

A generous person always gets their generosity back tenfold. And that's generosity of spirit as well as hard cash. Nobody likes a tightass or an emotional cripple, so be giving with money and feelings and show it. This also works the other way – you should receive generously as well, especially when your babe buys you something unexpected for your birthday.

You need to have knowledge

It's handy if you know the difference between Chardonnay and Chablis, a sorbet and the Sorbonne; where to get a cheap set of tyres, how to fix a dripping tap, who the Renaissance painters were and where the most romantic honeymoon spot on earth is. Men are supposed to know all manner of stuff (so keep absorbing everything – you'll get there).

You need to be worldly

This comes from having travelled, mixing with those who have or simply having a very open mind. You know where the best boutique hotels are in New York and Paris, where to shop in ten world capitals and what to buy where. More than that though, it means that you're not fazed when something untoward happens. You're measured but open to new ideas.

You need to be modest

Modesty is something many men have a problem with. They feel the need to scream from the rafters about even their most minuscule achievements. OK, so you won 'salesman of the year' last year or you're the reigning Olympic 200m sprint champion. It's the last thing you mention. It will surface eventually. Wait for the 'You didn't tell me that ...' when she finds out. And when she does, she will be doubly impressed.

You need to have clout

Clout is the personal leverage you have as a man. It's a measure of your ability to get the right table in a restaurant, or get a group of you past the nightclub bouncer without resorting to arrogance; a mature way of dealing with things, such as getting the waiter's attention without clicking your fingers and shouting, 'Hey, bring me the bill.' You should get the same result with a gentle nod of your head.

You need to be confident

This is the sum of all the others. Even if you only score big on six out of eleven, congratulations – that's more than most men.

Now get out there.

3
Where to find women

Get closer to the women you want

Research – do your homework

Once you recognise that there are millions of women out there who fit your profile, and you are aware of them, you need to get to know these women so that you can get closer to them and connect with them. Do your research properly and you can literally get inside the head of the woman you want – know her lifestyle, her habits, her topics of conversation, her background, her likes and dislikes, even her secret wishes.

Be warned though, this researching of a woman's behaviour can become obsessive – at which point this is called 'stalking', which is considered very unsocial behaviour. A little light snooping though can be very rewarding and can oil the wheels of a 'chance' meeting and subsequent seduction.

Talk to somebody who knows her well

Any snippet of insider information, however trivial, is meaningful and reveals something about her. She has a weakness for M&Ms; she always holidays in Greece; she's a lawyer and wants to be a partner; she wanted to dance but fell off her horse aged six; she speaks Japanese and was going to get married but her fiancé was zapped in an earthquake – every little snippet provides vital information about this woman's profile, her personality, the state of her mind and personal game plan. All of which means that you can more rapidly find the common denominator that brings you closer together.

Follow her

This may sound far too cloak-and-dagger for most, but if you follow anyone for an hour or so you will uncover unbelievable intelligence about them and be able to build a personal blueprint of that person. You would probably find out where they work, shop, eat, what car they drive, who their friends are, where they get their hair done, and surprising detail about their private lives. These details can provide a workable foundation on which to build a decent attacking game plan and give you the edge over other men.

Where to find women

The simple truth about women is: if you want to find a woman, look where the women are. This sounds like a no-brainer but you'd be surprised at the number of guys who go nowhere else but the local snooker club every night and stand at the bar scratching their heads wondering where the talent is: 'I never seem to meet any women.'

If you find yourself in a dark, smoky, boring old pool bar, night after night, cradling your pint of Webster's bitter like an old friend, probably your only friend, then it's time to radically change your habits. Women don't like hanging about in dark, smoky dives frequented by rough hairy-assed guys who sink pint after pint, play darts and whose only contribution to the conversation is the odd belch. They prefer being in light, airy fashionable places where they can show off their new clothes, their trendy hairstyle, latest Nokia and that Prada handbag (or fake copy) you bought her for her birthday. Girls like to see and be seen. They like to show off. They are social princesses.

Change your routine, often

Routine is boring, limits your outlook and restricts your exposure to a wider audience of women. If you do the same thing, day in and day out, you will only meet the same women again and again, whereas if you keep altering your behaviour pattern and routine, you will open yourself to meeting a new crop of women with every change. Keep altering your routine whether it's your route into work, the type of transport you take – bus one minute, tube the next, bike the next – the place where you park, the café where you get your sandwiches, the times that you do things. Keep changing your lifestyle and you will meet wave after wave of new women in normal, everyday situations.

20 simple strategies for meeting waves of new women

1. Go jogging or to the gym – regularly

Set the alarm early and get your togs on (preferably clean, fashionable ones). Pick a popular running route or a busy gym. The number of women who are wearing almost nothing and strutting their stuff at 6 a.m. is astonishing. Beware though, this is a slow burn. They hate being approached while red-faced and sweaty, so take it easy. Build up a rapport over a period of time with a smile and a non-threatening 'hi', and strike when an opportunity presents itself. Once you've made contact, however loose, you can build on that every time you see them. You'll suddenly start recognising many of these women outside the gym, when they aren't hot and sweaty and far more approachable.

2. Alter your appearance

Women respond to visual cues and have a set 'look' that catches their eye and triggers their response. It depends on your job of course, there's no point in getting fired, but, if you can, try and alter your appearance throughout the month. You may as well experiment with different personas and what effect they have on women. And I don't mean get a false nose and beard. Pick four distinct looks – the preppie look, the businessman, cool casual and the hip and happening. You'll be surprised how a different set of women will warm to one look or another and you will suddenly get noticed by a woman who would never have looked at you before.

3. Do one thing that you would never normally do in your lifetime

Do something that is so far out of your usual stratosphere that you get vertigo. For instance, go to the ballet. Don't laugh. It's full of millions of women and gay guys (for the most part). I don't care if you don't know the difference between a pas de deux and a padded cell, or *Swan Lake* and Swan Lager, just trust me. Get there and check it out. Your jaw will fall off. You will be astounded at the sheer volume of talent. Ditto:

gymnastics, ice skating, tennis, swimming or hockey tournaments (zillions of fit women).

4. Master the rising trot

Want to meet loads of hot women in tight pants and boots carrying whips? Get close to a horse. Whether it's the local stables or Royal Ascot, women love horses. They also love men who can ride them. It takes about half a dozen lessons before you feel comfortable with these four-legged lumps, but once you get your rising trot right, it doesn't matter what you look like – you suddenly enter the realm of 'dashing'. Women consider galloping along a remote stretch of beach, or heath, very sexy indeed. And the question 'Do you ride?' elicits sudden interest from most women and sends your conversation down a very intimate new course. They begin to see you very differently. And think about this: do you know how many women love riding whose husbands or partners aren't remotely interested? Visit your local stables and you'll notice that the odds are stacked very much in your favour, with about eight to ten women of all ages to every man.

5. Take out a personal ad

So, you work in an insurance company in a remote satellite office with no windows and ten grey-suited assessors, none of them cute? OK, there's a Girl Friday but she's married with kids. You feel stranded. What you need is a personal ad. Time was when personal columns smacked of desperation and had some sad sub-human stigma attached. These days, especially in Europe and America, personal ads are becoming a very fashionable and noble addition to the usual dating scene. The trick is to be as honest as possible (leave out the bit about your brush with the local constabulary on Christmas Eve) and aim locally. Make it convenient for you to meet. Internet smooching is easy, but when your hot date is in Phoenix, Arizona, the chances of her making it to Bradford Royal Theatre to catch a movie are slim. (See page 147 for an in-depth focus on personal ads.)

6. Get your morning coffee at a different place

Simple move, but very effective. Instead of the usual avocado and bacon sandwich at Luigi's, pick a different coffee bar near where you work every day. Then change your times. Try this café rotation for a month – I guarantee that between 7.30 and 8.30 a.m. you will probably see every woman who works in the vicinity, including that blonde who sped by in the MGB the other day. You'll know what each buys, what papers and magazines they read, how they react to the coffee-bar owner (smiley, chatty, surly) and where they go next. A casual 'She seems nice' to the eagle-eyed waiter will glean oceans of valuable information.

7. Check out the night classes

Women's magazines have been telling readers this nugget for years. But, do you know what? Nobody's been telling guys to go there as well. So, I'm telling you now. I started a course of Italian and couldn't believe my eyes – it was full of women and 60 per cent were reasonably tasty. In my class alone there were ten women and three guys, one of whom was gay. I lusted after at least three of the babes in my session. There were four different classes timetabled at the same time. That's four classes, 40 babes, 12 guys (four of whom were gay). You can't buy those odds. At the end of every session all four groups got together for a coffee and biscuit for a social 'cool down', and then we all crammed into the same lift to get to the ground floor. At the end of each term, we all had a party – 40 babes to eight straight guys. It was heaven.

8. Don't discount Weight Watchers

Another mate was sort of feeling low because he had a weight problem. His belly was heading south faster than the starlings in autumn. After much deliberation and not a little persuasion he reluctantly joined Weight Watchers, despite him thinking it was going to be hell – you know, carrot juice and lettuce – but instead he thought he'd died and gone to heaven. The place was crawling with women. Not only that, it was crawling with women who had the same problem and the same motivation that he had. And like him, half of them weren't *really* fat, they just needed a spot of discipline and motivation. Apart from anything else, get this: they applauded his 'manliness' for having the courage to admit he had a problem and they were doubly interested. In the classes he became a minor celebrity and his sex life went through the roof – he was literally fighting them off. By the time he'd lost a few pounds and could actually see his penis again, his confidence was sky high.

9. Traffic – road outrage

Women take on a different personality in their cars and are outrageous flirts. They love it. The car is a safety zone within which we are all more sexy, arrogant, pushy, angry and violent. We are all more daring in the car and women can be very responsive to a wave, a smile and some unorthodox behaviour (like letting them go first). Here you've got to be quick, be cheeky and use your brain.

Best use of the situation? A mate was in heavy traffic with a gorgeous babe one car behind him, creeping along. He checks her out in the mirror, she checks him back, and he detects a half smile. He does some playful dance with his hands through the sunroof. Not *that* funny but she laughs. He waves his business card at her and then opens his door and leaves his business card on the tarmac having first written on it: 'You are completely gorgeous – if you don't call me I won't be able to breathe tonight', or words to that effect. She creeps up to the card, opens her door, picks up the card. Smiles. He waves and disappears into the melée of late-model German saloons that is Hampstead. Next thing, there's a message waiting for him at work: 'GTi babe says call now' with her number. Invention and cheek are what get you noticed.

Write 'Call me, now' with your mobile number on a piece of card (in big numbers) and whenever you see a babe on a mobile phone, show her it. I know, it's obvious and a little crass, but don't knock it until you've tried it – you may be pleasantly surprised. You might want to pretend to be writing it before you lift it up.

> **NOTE:** *It always helps if you have a halfway decent car (see car sense, page 20).*

10. Go somewhere far away

Travel is romantic. Why? Because you never know what or who is around the next corner, you're away from everybody who knows your dark and lurid past, and, if need be, you can suitably embellish your life story to make it more exciting. You can tell little white lies about what you do and where you're from and how, next year, you're going to inherit the family chain of men's outfitters. Not that you would need to do this, of course.

It doesn't matter whether you're on a ferry crossing the Mersey, a plane to Florence, or the Eurostar to Paris, if there's a babe and she's headed your way, you've got more in common than most. People open up more to strangers and you can find yourself chatting away like old friends in less than an hour.

The trick is to convert this warm beginning into a blossoming relationship, or at least hot sex. Don't be so wet that you just shuffle off with that polite grin you see on so many just-landed planes – 'Bye then, have a good rest of your trip' – without getting her name, her address or hotel and a contact number. Don't let her out of your sight until you've got the lot. Chances are she's moving around or sightseeing, so get in touch that day. Just call her and say, 'Haven't been able to think of anything else since I got off the plane. Fancy dinner tonight? I'd love to carry on our conversation.'

11. Skiing – the ultimate snow job

Skiing is an aphrodisiac. An ability to ski well and a working knowledge of the best ski slopes and après ski culture in Europe and America should be a fundamental male skill. Skiing, whether or not you ever actually manage to get on the slopes, allows you to get a babe alone in a chalet in a fairy-tale valley surrounded by mountains where she can get a tan, and drink large amounts of glühwein in front of a log fire. If she doesn't melt into your arms in this situation she never will.

> **TIP:** *To start with go somewhere cheap and cheerful like Andorra in the Pyrenees. Andorra is basically one huge duty-free shop and is littered with spectacular talent, particularly university students, who get very drunk and become extremely experimental in the sex department.*

Once you've got your ski legs, work out what equipment you really need and what suits you and your pocket, and then hit the chic slopes of France and Switzerland, where in resorts like Courcheval or Gstaad everything is five times the price and the women are slightly more aristocratic, but no less horny, especially after a jug or two of *vin chaud*.

12. Take flying lessons, and take advantage of women's weakness for pilots

No, you're right, you don't meet any women in the back of a two-seater Cessna, but you'd be surprised at how impressed women still are with the word 'pilot'. The fact that a commercial pilot these days is nothing more than a glorified taxi driver is way beyond them, so you may as well make the fantasy work for you. Women love pilots and the ability to fly conjures up all sorts of romantic ideas in their heads. Apart from anything else, flying a plane is a cool skill to have – especially if you're on your way to Aintree for the Grand National with the lads in a small plane and your pilot suddenly has a heart attack. The headline 'Six Execs Die in Air Crash' is suddenly replaced by 'Hero Race Fan Saves Six Lives' thanks to your quick thinking, and you can bask in the glory for years. But also, once you have your licence and join a flying club you can feasibly borrow a plane and nip across the channel to Le Touquet for a dirty weekend at the Westminster Hotel. This goes down very well. Especially when your babe gets to the office on Monday morning and somebody says, 'Did you have a nice weekend?' Did she ever.

> **TIP:** *You can spend a fortune on the odd lesson here and there but the problem with the UK is the weather. If you're really interested it's best to take three weeks off and go to air school in Florida or South Africa where it's cheap, the instruction is first class and the weather and your licence are more or less guaranteed.*

13. Relax at the spa

If you want to meet well-tended rich women with time on their hands, book yourself into a wellness spa for the day.

Anyone can join in if you can afford the hundred quid or so for the day and a handful of treatments.

There are half-naked women of all ages wandering about in towelling robes getting pampered and taking advantage of various beauty and relaxation therapies, and it's easy to get chatting by the pool or in the sauna.

Women are very receptive to company away from their busy, stressful lives – and husbands – and it can get quite stale and boring in between treatments. Consequently the women can become uncharacteristically playful and mischievous once they've flicked through last month's *Vogue* and *Tatler* for the fifteenth time. If you're unfortunate to pick a slow day, at least you will get a decent massage from that fragrant blonde in a white coat. May as well get your nails manicured as well while no-one is looking.

> **TIP 1:** *Go somewhere where they encourage active relaxation as opposed to a traditional health farm with the whole stereotypical nuts-and-carrot juice, weight-loss routine.*

> **TIP 2:** *Be sensitive to her situation. She may be feeling a little dazed and floaty after a massage or facial. In which case offer to pour her a glass of water.*

> **NOTE:** *Health farms are for fatties, wellness centres are for wealthy, stressed-out babes who look after their bodies and looks, and love being pampered.*

14. Do anything dangerous

Women are getting braver by the minute and are embracing all sorts of extreme and dangerous pursuits from rock-climbing, paragliding and bungee jumping, to kayaking and sky-diving, in an attempt to push their personal limit. And they are not all those dowdy, rugged, weather-beaten, worthy adventurers of old you used to see hiking up Ben Nevis as a kid. Get involved in any kind of adventure sport and you will meet a steady stream of young, fit, attractive and interesting women. They are tasty, fashionable, switched-on babes who hunger for the thrills and excitement that danger provides, since danger is a natural aphrodisiac. The thing about danger is it provides an endorphin rush that is semi-orgasmic and intrinsically sexual.

Have you ever been near a woman when she's just passed her driving test? At that moment she is so erotically charged she could probably shag the decrepit 65-year-old test assessor. When you both land safely on an airstrip, after your first 'jump' together from 10,000 feet, you are flushed with the same feeling. You are both on such a high, due to having just cheated death, you can't help but hug and kiss each other – repeatedly. The sheer act of experiencing something life-threatening together conspires to bring you closer together. Even if you stay in and watch a scary movie together – the same principle applies. So get dangerous.

> **NOTE:** *Women who love adventure outside the bedroom generally love adventure inside it. In fact, forget the bedroom.*

15. Get a market stall

Have you noticed how many young single women are browsing around market stalls on a Saturday and Sunday morning? Of course they're curious and keen to spot a bargain, but ask your-self this: why are they on their own on a weekend morning when they should be sharing a *petit pain chocolat* and cappuc-cino with their lover after a heavy night of passion? Either the man in their life is a baker or retailer or they haven't got a man in their life. Choose something to sell that you're genuinely interested in and when that delectable babe wanders around your stall you can be sure she's interested in the same thing as you. You can astound her with your knowledge of eighteenth-century silverware or pop art. If you've got no imagination whatsoever, you can always flog second-hand CDs.

16. Join a decent tennis club

Want to see lots of girls in short skirts and frilly underwear with tight caramel thighs? Join a tennis club. They're always one short for doubles and it's very easy to get talking after a game, when everyone is chilling out with a Coke or a glass of Pimms. Spending a long lazy summer afternoon knocking a ball about is very sexy, and tennis is incredibly intimate and accessible, unlike squash where players are penned in, or golf, where the women tend to disappear with each other and you're stuck with other guys. Watch how many fabulous women turn out for the local tournament.

17. Join a band or become a photographer

I remember reading an interview with Bob Geldof where he said that he only joined a band to get laid. Groupies start at local level and it doesn't matter what instrument you play (OK, forget the triangle), or what style of music, at what venue – if you're on stage and they're not, you are assured of some after-gig attention.

It's the same with photographers. I've never met a photog-rapher yet whose sole motive for becoming one was anything other than getting women to take their clothes off. And these days, with digital cameras, even a chimpanzee can take a decent picture. At first it's slightly nerve-wracking but you soon get the hang of it. As editor of *Playboy* I always had to ask the models to take their kit off, even ex-Miss Worlds. You have to check because models are notorious liars – about their age, their size, what's in their portfolio, etc. What surprised me – pleasantly – was the speed with which they complied.

18. Speak publicly

If you've got any kind of skill or talent that you can pass on, or have done something extraordinary recently like scale Everest or snapped the lesser-spotted grebe-warbler, then there are any number of women's groups who are desperate for decent-looking guys to address them. Don't wait for them to come to you – they'll never think of it – but check the local businesswomen's guild, or whatever, and offer your services. Being on stage in front of a captive audience of women will give you ample opportunity to survey the talent and while you're rambling on you can decide who to target at the after-talk drinks. Even the local Women's Institute will have one decent woman in it.

> **TIP:** *Make it funny.*

19. Get a part-time job as a barman

I know you're never going to make hairdresser, shoe salesman or lingerie salesmen, so the next best thing is a barman. Choose carefully, though. You need to find a swish bar or hotel where classy women hang out and where it isn't unusual for single women to pop in for a drink. You only need to work two nights a week but make sure they are the busiest nights. This may seem a trifle déclassé if you're the CEO of Daimler-Benz, but the change of pace might do you good. It pays badly but your social life is taken care of for the evening, and you do meet a steady flow of new women who feel strangely at ease talking to you. Once she finds out that you're only doing this until your film script sells or your bond-dealer licence comes through, she will be suitably intrigued.

20. Get a dog

If all else fails, get a dog. Anything that barks or has floppy ears, particularly when it's at the puppy stage, is a babe magnet. You must have seen *101 Dalmations* – boy with dog meets girl with dog. Clean the dog, go and sit in your local park on a sunny afternoon and wait. It works every time.

The usual suspects (don't overlook the obvious)

Office affairs

It's a classic case of ignoring the obvious, but there are many men and women who stubbornly ignore the opportunity to form a relationship with somebody at work because a) they feel uncomfortable doing so, b) they don't think it ethically right, c) they are afraid of what other people might say, or d) they think it will spoil their chances of promotion.

The problem here, of course, is that you spend half your life at work and the chances are there are some very tasty women who inhabit your office, some of whom you would certainly fantasise about having sex with, if not quite getting married to. To turn your back on a steady talent stream of attractive women for the aforementioned reasons is a depressing thought and should not be entertained if your right woman suddenly pops into view across the open-plan cubicles.

Although here there are rules to abide by if you are to maintain a good sexual and working relationship with the woman.

- **Don't tell anyone.** At least one other person will inevitably find out but keep your secret between as few people as possible. That way, if things do turn sour or go belly up the entire office won't take sides. Once the office knows, someone will set about sabotaging your relationship either by rumour-mongering or other devious means.

- **Make a pact.** If you do break up in the future neither of you will use it against the other in the work environment.

- **Have sex privately.** Keep any smooching, sweet-talking, snogging and passionate e-mails and notes out of the office, and don't get caught shagging in the storeroom. Control yourself.

Nightclubs

The local nightclub is where most of the local talent of a specific age usually end up after a night out drinking. Consequently, it's where most men get started with women.

Nightclubs are terrible places to meet women unless you are the classic 'tall, dark and handsome' and can actually dance really well. It certainly isn't the right place for short, bald fatties with glasses – no matter how many bottles of champagne you can afford.

Nightclubs can frighten many men. First of all you have to get past the bouncers and once inside it's dark, you can't hear each other speak, you have to dress in an extrovert manner to get noticed and you have to dance, which many men find excruciatingly painful and embarrassing. Also, if you're over 35 you stick out like a spare prick at a wedding – unless, of course, you're the one in the Stringfellows booth buying Bollinger at £250 a bottle surrounded by Page 3 girls and gossip columnists.

Weddings

There is something extraordinarily aphrodisiac about a wedding and they are terrific places to meet women. Romance is in the air, everyone is incredibly relaxed, friendly and well dressed (some with garters), and out for a good time at somebody else's huge expense. There's always an abundance of 'old friends' that you haven't seen for a while and 'new friends' who you can quickly get to know. Weddings are incredibly sexy events. Everybody has some tenuous link with everybody else so you can ask the bridesmaid about her tasty best mate from college who she hasn't seen in six years. Also, weddings usually soak up oceans of alcohol and the women always end up in a very flirty and sexy mood. Dancing is part of the required agenda so you can get up close and personal very fast. Just try not to get caught with your pants down in the church rhododendrons with somebody else's wife. And try not to get caught looking after some ageing aunt who might be sweet but will distract you from the job at hand.

> **TIP:** *Don't be afraid of going to a wedding alone. In fact, I actively encourage it. The women will take you to their bosom – which is precisely where you want to be.*

Funerals

At the risk of sounding sick and taking advantage of your great-uncle Ernie's untimely misfortune, the funeral, like the wedding, can be an opportunist's dream. There's always one dishy babe who you've never seen before or haven't seen in a while – 'Sandra, haven't seen you for ages, you look fantastic.' Everyone feels obliged to talk to one another, women always look terrific in black and it's a scientific fact that death stimulates our hormones to want to mate and repopulate the planet. Why disappoint them? Once the glum ceremony is over, the after-party can be surprisingly buoyant and any welcome alcohol makes it easy to suggest moving on to somewhere less macabre where you can rest with your piece.

WORKSHOP 1
How to pick up a great woman in a strange bar

On your next business trip to a new town, don't be stuck in your hotel with a cold room, dodgy remote and a knocking radiator. Get out and meet someone, preferably female.

So you've arrived in a strange town on business and you may as well be on Mars, except the good news is the local population have one head, look the same as you and talk your language. Your business associates are too lazy or distracted to pick you up from the airport and show you around so you're on your own. But you can't bear the thought of another lonely night surrounded by lacklustre hotel staff, sipping five-quid-a-pop malt whiskey across the bar from a barman with the conversational agility of Sly Stallone. You've seen all the videos – even the naughty ones. What you need is some action. Women. But how? Where? Don't despair, this is a fantastic opportunity.

Don't waste any time
On the way to your hotel from the airport drain the taxi driver of every morsel of information about bars, clubs and happenings in his town: where the women go and what they're like – snooty, friendly, trendy? You might need to read between the lines since the average taxi driver's idea of a hot spot could be a boil on the back of his neck. If you're renting a car pick the brains of that delightful, charming Avis

babe with the constant toothpaste-commercial smile. Can she suggest a bar that throbs? A restaurant that has a certain ambiance? A café that is teeming with talent? Does she want to join you? Of course not – what a silly question. Has she got a sister? Before leaving the airport, pick up a local paper. You don't want to wake up tomorrow and find out that the Vogue Model of the Year contest was hosted in the town and you missed the post-competition party just 100 metres from your hotel.

Look the part

In your hotel room, instead of doing what everybody else does – turning on the telly and cruising the channels, trying out the bed, checking out the bathroom and the shower cap, brand of shampoo and bathing foam – get naked, take a shower and get out of your business suit.

> **TIP:** *Always carry a decent, clean, casual jacket (Boss or Armani if you can afford it, Next if you can't), a good pair of chinos or designer jeans and a casual shirt. Avoid the temptation to unbutton it to the waist and please leave the medallion at home. Have a shave, splash on some Eau Sauvage, stop by the cash machine to fill up your wallet and you're off on a wild adventure.*

Reconnaissance

Avoid the temptation to dive into the first place that looks remotely light and warm. You have to seek out the right joint to find the right type of woman with whom you're usually compatible. Over 35s should avoid places that sound and look like an 18–24 singles holiday. Check out the places for visual indicators like ambiance, décor, the way people are dressed, the music they play and the volume they play it.

What time does it cook?

Once you've located the right place, find out what time it gets going. All bars have a time when they are hot. Too early or late and you miss the best babes who either haven't arrived or have moved on somewhere else. Once you know, get there slightly early to claim your spot at the bar or wherever. The fact that people arrive after you means that they will respect your space and acknowledge your domain. Arrive too late and other people will have settled in every decent spot. Your arrival will be an infringement on their space and you will be seen and treated as an unwelcome interloper; which means that you will be relegated to the back room.

Don't be shy

Pick a spot in the middle of the bar with all-around visibility and a good view of the ladies' toilet. You don't want to miss anyone. With your first drink tip the bar person very well or offer to buy them a drink and build a rapport. This will come in handy later when you need to display your skill at getting a drink at a crowded bar. Once you've made sure you're not standing in the favourite spot of the local bruiser, relax and make like you own the joint.

Build up your confidence

Yes, you're on your own but just because you are on your own doesn't mean that you should look lonely or sorry for yourself. You're not a dork. During those early moments, as the bar begins to fill, start building your own confidence. Check out the people as they arrive. All right, half of them are couples but how many of them are happy? (A UK study showed that 45 per cent of women are with men they don't really want to be with.) OK, that guy in the corner is Mr Good-Looking but he hasn't said a word to his girlfriend since they arrived. They've obviously just had a fight. The group of people on the big table look like an office party, or else it's someone's birthday. They're having fun but how many of them will be going home with each other? Very few people have inter-office affairs these days and those that do keep it very quiet. They're drinking like Fleet Street hacks; when they start getting rowdy and brave you can move in. Get in the mood. Hey, you're an attractive guy. Things are looking up. Look, it isn't *that* serious. If you hit it off with someone, great – if not at least you've had an entertaining evening. And woman-watching is far preferable to watching a movie. It's sport.

Observe

Don't hunch over the bar with your back to the action like Quasimodo – turn around and face the crowd like you're the hottest gunslinger in town. Don't stare. Just casually trickle your eyes over the joint in a wide sweep. When you get flashed an interesting or encouraging smile from that blonde in the corner, smile back; but take it easy – don't rush over there and stick your tongue down her throat. Patience is the key. You may not have much time in the town but rushing is a sign of desperation and women can smell desperation from 20 miles. And it's very, very ugly. Keep your eye on her and after the third smile or when a suitable opportunity presents itself, move over and chat. Say, 'I can't resist your smile.'

Take control of the bar

As the place fills up, you are in a perfect position to control the ebb and flow of who goes to and from the bar, in what order, in your domain. Wait until a woman wants to get to the bar – there will be a steady stream throughout the night – and step aside. Make space for her, deliberately, so she cannot notice.

TRICK 1: *Just as men can't iron, women are useless at getting drinks at bars. You will have already made a mate of the barman/woman so when you see a decent woman struggling to get a drink, simply raise your hand at the barman (never flick your fingers), nod and he will get to you sooner rather than later. When he does, pass him over to the lady ('Can you get her a drink, please?'). She will be impressed, invariably thank you and we now have conversation. So talk.*

TRICK 2: *Let's say you fancy the girl in the red dress and her mate in the yellow dress comes to get the drinks. Say something like, 'Excuse me, but your friend in the red dress, is she with anyone?' Women love this conspiratorial tone and she'll certainly give you the form – in triplicate – while she's waiting for the drink. In fact you probably won't be able to get rid of her, which may or may not be a blessing. Before she disappears, remind her that you're interested in Ms Red Dress. She will hurry back to the group and tell her all about this charming man (you are, aren't you?) who fancies her like mad. If nothing happens at least you've got half the bar talking about you. But make it happen.*

Know the weak spots

There are certain moments throughout an evening when women are neglected and socially vulnerable, even those with men. It's frightening how many men literally ignore their partners all night as they bang on about something to a mate, play pool or flirt with somebody else. Look for the woman in the group who looks left out. There's always one. The one with the weak smile who's obviously not enjoying herself. She's uncomfortable, fidgety, keeps looking around and looks slightly embarrassed. She needs rescuing. Her body language is screaming 'GET ME OUT OF HERE!' Pick up on it. Get into her vibe. Get close to her and then, if you get talking, suggest you go somewhere quieter for a coffee. Or pass her your business card with your mobile number on it and say call me now. It's old-fashioned but it works. The fact that you actually noticed her discomfort will have her reeling back in shock.

Intercept her

When she goes to the toilet, intercept her by going at the same time. Smile and say 'Hi. Excuse me, but are you with that guy?' You'll be surprised at the response which could be any of: 'Yes, but I wish I wasn't', 'Oh, he's just a friend' or 'No, that's my brother.' Anything halfway positive means Game On! Just be blunt and tell her what you feel. 'Look, I think you're gorgeous and would love to meet you sometime.' Give her your business card, but don't depend on her to call. 'Can I call you?' Write down her number and call her when you get back to your place at the bar.

> **NOTE:** *Never insult the guy she's with ('Are you really with that prick?') or she'll think you're arrogant and will feel the need to start defending him. Insult him and you're insulting her choice of men. Not a good move if you want to be the next one.*

A right pair

Don't try and split up two women. With women, there's always a great-looking one and a not-so-great-looking one, a fat one and a thin one … don't ask. This is simply the nature of two women together. Don't even think about shutting out the not-so-great-looking one because she will then set about sabotaging any move you make with the gorgeous one. She'll yawn at your humour, look at her watch and criticise your appearance. Now if you start

chatting up the not-so-great-looking one first, completely ignoring the sex goddess, then once the hot babe picks herself up
from the floor (remember that this does not happen very often),
then instead of sabotaging the relationship, she will feel the need
to compete in order to reassert her rightful place in the pecking
order, i.e. First Princess. Consequently, when the ugly one goes to
the toilet, or to get a round of drinks which she has to do at
least once in the evening, the hot babe will be all over you like a
rash. Grab her telephone number before the other one gets back.

Always be responsive

During the evening, wherever you are, you will definitely get
chatted up by at least one woman. Especially as they get drunker
and braver. It might be something ordinary like her asking the
time or wanting to get past, it could be just playful banter, or
she might just fancy you, lucky boy, and say her personal version
of 'What's a nice boy like you doing in a place like this?' It's a big
step for a woman to talk to you first. Respect this. Remember
that women think they are being forward when they're breathing
in the same room. But if you find a woman sticking her firm
breasts into your back or side you can correctly assume that she's
marginally interested. Some women – even very young ones –
will be surprisingly motherly: 'What are you doing here alone?' At
this point, don't get all defensive and say, 'I'm not really a sad
bastard – I'm a nice guy with lots of friends, honest', and never
ever give a straight answer. Best course is to be self-deprecating.
Smile and say, with a twinkle in your eye, 'Yes, it's very sad. I
used to have lots of friends but what with the bad breath and
boring conversation ...' If you're brave you might say something
mischievous (with the appropriate cheeky look) like, 'You see the
problem is, I'm lousy in bed' which is a fantastic catalyst to move
on to the subject of sex. In this scenario it's interesting how
women will often defend you ('You can't be that bad, surely?').

Should she say anything like, "What you need is more practice', bingo. Of course, if she's a complete lump and you don't fancy her it still pays to be civil and funny. Her mate might just be gorgeous and lonely.

4
The approach

The theory is all very well but there comes a time when you have to put theory into practice and put your balls on the line. It's easy to talk strategies and predict various scenarios and outcomes but there is no substitute for going out there and doing it, and there is nobody else who can do it for you. You need to make it happen.

Rejection – it's just a learning process

Before we get into the pitch, and moving in on the woman of your choice, let's deal with the harrowing subject of rejection, which is the single biggest fear factor that inhibits men from making a move on a woman. But how serious is it? If you get a 'no', take it on the chin and move on. It wasn't to be – so what? Half the time rejection is really only in your own head and it really isn't that serious. The trick is to learn from any mistakes you make and refine your approach. I've spoken to hundreds of women on the subject, young and old, and they all said practically the same thing.

The eight classic mistakes women say men make

1. **'Some men are rejecting themselves even as they are asking me out.'**
   If you find yourself saying self-destructive phrases like 'I know you probably wouldn't want to, but I'd really like to take you out one night', then stop it right away. Duh! You may as well draw a target on your forehead and hand her a crossbow. First of all, how do you know what she is thinking? She may actually adore you. In an attempt to pre-empt rejection you are actively encouraging it and it becomes a self-fulfilling prophecy. You've got 'LOSER' written all over you.

> **TIP:** *When asking a woman out, always put the emphasis on her, and how fabulous she is – not how bad you think you are.*

2. **'I hate men who apologise for asking me out.'**
   Don't apologise. Some men say sorry for everything. If you could hear a tape-recording of yourself you probably say sorry a million times a day. Stop yourself. Get out of the habit of saying sorry. Asking a woman out is not a hindrance or a waste of time – you're not trying to sell her a timeshare, you're offering her a legitimate golden

opportunity to partake in the rest of your life. That's quite an offer.

3. **'I'd rather go out with an ugly, confident man than a good-looking nervous wreck.'**
   If a terrific-looking woman came up to you perspiring and red-faced, and started blurting out an incoherent string of sentences about how she wanted to seduce you, you'd think she was a basket case, make your excuses and leave. It's the same in reverse.

4. **'I don't think men understand timing. There are times when I'm not interested in having a man talk to me and times when I am.'**
   Of course, working this out is practically impossible but there are certain guidelines: avoid approaching a woman when she's in the middle of something strenuous, private, or what could be construed as a girlie moment, or when she is not looking her best and trying to hide from the public glare.

5. **'I wish men would think about the woman they're talking to and target themselves more accurately; they should ask women out who might at least say "maybe". I get the feeling that most men just ask out every woman with two legs and two tits and hope for the best.'**
   So avoid the scatter-gun approach – the art of marketing yourself properly and tailoring your delivery to one kind of woman or another who fall into your attraction bracket, and not trying to shag everything on the planet that has a pulse.

6. **'I hate men who are over-familiar right away.'**
   What she means are those men who slap her on the back and kiss her on the cheek in a social kiss before being formally introduced.

7. **'What irritates me are those men who think they are God's gift to women.'**
   What she means are those arrogant bastards who think that they'll score just by turning up. So you can be over-confident bordering on smug. Smug never goes down well with anybody or in any situation, whether it's with a woman or not.

8. **'I hate those men who barge into you and crowd you with their body.'**
   Many women talk about the physical space invaders – those men who literally invade their body space and deliberately barge their bodies into them when talking to them.

Why she might reject you

She may just loathe the sight of you and think you a complete slimeball or bonehead, whatever *she* looks like (her loss), but there are many other legitimate reasons why a woman might reject you out of hand – and these don't include the obvious one that she's 'taken' already:

- **You might have just caught her completely off-guard** and she doesn't quite know how to deal with the situation. She wasn't expecting to be swept off her feet and a quick 'thanks, but no thanks' stops her having to think about it and make a decision in what, for her, is an uncomfortable situation. She may regret it the minute you walk away, but too late, you're history.

> **TIP:** *You might want to pre-empt that by giving her your business card and saying, 'If you ever change your mind, please give me a call.'*

- **She may not be in the mood** for a number of reasons: her car has just been broken into; she's not feeling well and has just thrown up; her boss has just called to say she's lost the IBM contract; she's just blown £10, 000 at the roulette table.

- **She might actually prefer women**, does not feel like explaining and doesn't want to get caught up in a caustic gender debate since lesbians generally attract quite hostile comments from rejected 'homophobic' men. When faced with a woman who says, 'Sorry, I'm a lesbian', try and avoid the temptation to say something crass like, 'That's interesting – can I watch?' or 'So am I'. Rather smile and say, 'I'm jealous – she's a very lucky woman' and leave it at that. You will have made a good friend.

- **Women need a lot of prep work** – the hair, the make-up, clean panties, fresh clothes, a dash of Opium – before they feel good about flirting and engaging in any kind of courtship ritual. Consequently even though she looks beautiful to you, if she thinks her hair or whatever looks like shit, she will try and get out of the way sooner rather than later. And she will constantly be worrying about minor style details while you are delivering your pitch. This distraction could be interpreted by you as 'not interested at all', when what she really means is 'Try me again later when I've had a bath.'

- **She may be experiencing female downtime.** Either hormonal or biological swings have altered her mood or well-being, and she just doesn't feel like it at the moment. You could find the next day that the same woman sparkles with openness. Keep trying.

Softening her resistance

Positive positioning

A positive approach means that you walk tall and full without slouching. Keep your shoulders big and straight without trying to look like a bodybuilder, sucking your stomach in or sticking your chest out like a robin redbreast. Just walk. Try and avoid the pimp-roll or any kind of marching.

Smile confidently, not that nervous half-smile that you used to show the headmaster when you got caught smoking at school.

Look into her eyes with a warm, genuine optimism – if you stare you will come over as challenging and she'll think you've got something to hide. If you look down, or anywhere but at her, she'll think you're a shady character with low self-esteem.

Keep your hands out of your pockets and stand close enough to her to be intimate – i.e. hear what she's saying – without crowding her private space or touching any of her private parts, especially her breasts and ass.

When talking to a woman don't fidget or scuff the ground with your toes and fiddle with parts of your clothing or any body parts. This smacks of a lack of confidence. And, I know this is a tough one, but resist the urge to scratch your balls. You're not a baboon.

Offer her easy terms

To 'seduce' means to slowly entice and engage, and basically tickle her fancy and get her going a bit before you hit her with the hard sell. You have to allow her to witness some of your benefits and how they affect her, before you make your pitch. Let her see that you are funny, clever, sexy and comfortable to be around.

Also, like any product, it's much easier for her if you offer her easy terms. A car salesman will never say 'Right sir, your Audi TT is road ready. That's thirty-three thousand quid. Can I have that in cash right now.' Instead he offers you hire purchase through a finance institution. And if he didn't no-one would ever buy a car. They couldn't afford to.

So they offer you easy terms – payment in instalments. Equally, it isn't advisable to just walk up to a woman and ask her out cold. You need to warm her up and you can't just blurt out something like 'Will you go out with me?' or the usual 'I was wondering if you would go out with me' – this is far too abrupt and represents much too high a personal commitment straight away. You have to ease her into it with juicy and enticing incremental instalments. Better to say, 'I've really enjoyed talking to you. Would you like to grab a bite to eat some time?' And once you've got an initial commitment, build on that.

Take the pressure off

It's often easier to gently get her used to you by inviting her along to something juicy and enticing with a group of (trusted) friends. She will see how you interact with other people and, hopefully, how they respect you. It's far less threatening to say casually, 'A group of us are going down to the Madonna concert/polo/ Formula 1/the big game, this Saturday – would you like to come along?' You can add something like 'I'll make sure you get back safely, before your bedtime' to assure her that you will be her escort and take responsibility for her.

> **TIP:** *Your friends are an extension of your personality, so make sure this group of friends know how to behave themselves and aren't going to get completely trashed and start flirting with her or saying juvenile things l ke 'My friend fancies you' or 'Have you slept together yet?' Pick the right*

friends and they can do a fantastic PR job for you. If a smart girl 'friend' sits with her for a quiet girlie chat and says something like 'He's a really fantastic guy – I know he's really keen on you', then she's doing your work for you.

Give her your confidence

If you're confident, she will be too. Confidence is intoxicating and catching. Everyone wants to be around positive, upbeat, confident people who are going places and doing interesting things. So if you can inspire and invigorate her with your enthusiasm towards her and about yourself, she will quickly catch the buzz and get hooked on it.

Find out if she is available, sooner rather than later

Once you've got over the hurdle of actually chatting to a woman, you can waste hours getting on famously with her and only then find out that she is happily married with three kids and has to catch a cab home in ten minutes to her house in Harrow. What a let-down! Try and establish early on what her marital or other status is, otherwise she will go home flattered by the interest and randy as hell for her husband to enjoy, whereas you will go home alone, exhausted and dejected. Don't do this to yourself.

Always get her telephone number

Whatever the situation you meet a woman in, don't leave without getting her name and a contact number, even if you're only half interested. When the clock strikes seven o'clock and you've nowhere to go that evening, and no-one to go anywhere with, I guarantee that she will seem slightly more appealing by the minute. Time and time again, men do all the prep work to perfection – chatting her up, warming her up, touching her arm, etc. – and then they reach the moment of truth and don't know how to close the deal ('Well, see you then'). And they disappear never to contact her again. Quitter!

Be your own man
Don't be afraid of going out alone – in fact try and do more of it. Going solo is the best way to meet women because you are forced to talk to someone you don't know. Communicating is an innate human instinct. So rather than huddle all night over a drink with your mate saying things like, 'I don't like yours much' or 'Bloody hell, look at that', and then go home alone, you will actually confront the opportunity. Go to that club or that event alone, if need be. You will be astounded at your change in attitude and the results.

He who hesitates
One of my mother's favourite sayings used to be 'He who hesitates is lost', and she used to repeat it so often she drove me nuts (bless her). The annoying thing is – she was right! How many times have you been in a situation where you've spotted some fabulous woman and just while you were psyching yourself up to approach her she either disappeared or somebody else moved in? How many 'right women' have you let get away? What if she was the one? I read a more modern version of the same saying on a website: 'He who hesitates, masturbates', which I thought even more apt.

Timing is everything
'If you'd asked me only last week I would have said yes, I really would, but I've just met this great guy and I couldn't. I've committed myself.'

Sometimes you're lucky, sometimes not so lucky. In our

high-speed world where a connection hinges on what you make of the briefest of encounters, a split second either way could be crucial. Luck, fate, destiny and all of those intangible forces often seem to conspire against you or can offer a pleasant surprise. The trick is to try and make your own luck by better reading of the situation, and more importantly, knowing the women you seek to engage with.

Gauging a woman's mood

You can blow a possible close encounter by performing the right approach at the wrong time. Knowing when to strike is crucial. There are times when a woman is on top of her game – she's gregarious, confident, fun, and the life and soul of any party. Then there are the times when you catch her at a low ebb – she's depressed, miserable and unconfident, and thinks and feels herself unattractive.

Be aware of your own mood swings

If you're in a bad mood, depressed, feeling negative or down for whatever reason, then this is not a good time to approach a woman. You need to be on top of your game, feeling up and positive. The more enthusiasm and passion, and the happier the vibe you can bring to your approach, the better it's going to work. Try and seduce a woman when your mind is elsewhere, and you may as well paint 'LOSER' on your forehead. Take time out, have a good sleep and get over it.

Just friends – the power of a girl 'friend'

If, when you lay your heart on the line, a woman says she likes you and thinks you are sweet (is there ever a worse adjective to be labelled with than sweet?) but wants to be 'just friends', then this to me is the biggest let-down ever. You've got friends, dozens of them, acquaintances coming out of your ears – what you don't need is more. You haven't got time to service the ones you've got. What you want is a lover.

However, don't dismiss this out of hand. Cultivate this relationship because a) she may change her mind when she realises how fantastic a guy you really are, and b) girl 'friends', whether real or just good friends, lead to other girlfriends (see Turning a girl 'friend' into a lover, page 88).

The other thing about having a girlfriend – even a casual one – is that you can use this as an excuse to *not* make a move on that delicious girl down the road who you really fancy like mad. If that sounds like reverse logic, you're right, it is. Let me explain. Maybe you fancy the girl down the road – let's call her Susan. The fact that you're unable to go out with Susan makes her safe for you to say suggestive and personal things to her and warm her up for when you can. 'I think you're terrific. If I wasn't going out with Sally I'd be after you like a shot. You're a very attractive woman …' You can get away with murder, and comfortably so, because already having a girlfriend gives you a convenient buffer. By the time you've finished teasing Susan mercilessly she will be desperate for you to drop Sally.

> **TIP:** *Always treat Sally honourably in Susan's eyes or you will lose her respect. Only when you feel that Susan is on the brink should you drop Sally. But then put the emphasis on Sally having left you to evoke the sympathy card and clear the way for Susan to jump in.*

By the same token, if she already has a boyfriend

OK, so this is the scenario: you fancy this woman but know that she is going out with somebody else who isn't one of your mates. This is the perfect opportunity to sell yourself to this woman in a 'safe' situation. You know you will be rejected because she already has a relationship, so the excuse factor is there, but this creates a safety zone where you can be much more suggestive and blunt than normal. The rejection itself is a soft-landing rejection since it's not because she hates you, it's because she can't go out with you, at the moment.

For example, what you're really saying is, 'I know you're going out with somebody else – I respect that; but I fancy you and if your circumstances should change then I'd be very interested in going out with you.' This is a win-win situation for her. She's flattered by the interest and she now knows that should her relationship turn sour, she's got an escape plan – a very intoxicating position to be in. Use this situation to say all of those personal things that you might ordinarily have difficulty blurting out.

Tell her you can't have sex

Want to make yourself instantly attractive to the opposite sex? Tell them you're not interested in sex, or have taken a vow of celibacy, or have bet your mate that you can do without sex for six months. This sounds churlish, almost childish, but is like a red rag to a bull. Women will see this as a challenge to their womanly wiles and will set about trying to seduce you and break your resolve. I mean, how could any man refuse to have sex with her, bet or no bet?

By removing the very thing that she's expecting, i.e. you trying to get inside her knickers as fast as possible, you've taken the wind out of her sails and put the ball well and truly back in her court. If she's interested then you've given her permission to set the pace. If she's not quite sure yet then you've allowed her the space she needs. A win-win situation.

NOTE: *Be warned though. The downside of this is that they may think that you aren't having sex because you have a dose of something untoward in the penis department, which is not an attractive thought.*

Avoiding the desperation trap

You look around and every other man seems to be hitting it off with fabulous sexy women with ease. You're not. Not only that – it's been ages and you're getting desperate. Will you ever talk to a woman, let alone kiss one, again? Things are seemingly desperate and that's not where you want to be, since women can smell it a mile off – they have an in-built desperation detector.

When you're desperate you tend to go overboard with various little details that the non-desperate man takes in his stride. For instance, desperadoes dress for a date as if it's their wedding. It may be your big night but don't overdo the 'formal clothes'. It's a date, not a job interview. Be more yourself. Maybe just tidy yourself up a bit.

If you can smell your aftershave in the next town, this signals that you are trying far too hard. Even an expensive, delicious, sexy aftershave needs to have subtle tones, and can leave a woman reeling in disgust if over-applied. The trick is to get her to want to lean closer in towards you to smell its sexual aroma, not to back off and run to the nearest army surplus store to get a gas mask.

TIP: *To get just the right amount of aftershave, do what sophisticated women do – spray the fragrance into the air in front of you and walk into it.*

When we're desperate we tend to overdo the chivalry and gallant knight act, leaping about like a mad bastard opening car doors and restaurant doors, pulling her coat off before she's unbuttoned it, buying her drinks, clearing her plate, and generally tugging your forelock. Anything to please. Yes, women like a gentleman, but not a doormat.

And have you heard yourself speak? Desperate men tend to rant on and give the woman a non-stop sales pitch, overpowering them with a barrage of words. Either they are over-complimentary about the woman and over-zealous about themselves, or both. It's as if they haven't spoken to anyone in the past year.

Calm down and relax

Conversation is a two-way street so let her get a word in. Give her the modicum of leverage, i.e. ask her a few open-ended questions, and then once she's off and running listen to her. Really listen. Let the silences work for you. Listen to what she has to say. And look at her face, not her breasts, as she's saying it.

> **TIP:** *Never ever admit that you haven't had a relationship for six months or over. Keep it loose and goosy. Intrigue her. Tell her that your last girlfriend had to relocate to Spain for her job and you tried commuting but it didn't work out. You hate paella. If you tell her that she met some Spanish news reporter, you will collect a sympathy vote.*

How to touch the untouchable

On a local level there's that babe who comes into the pub twice a week – a real stunner and a local 'celebrity'. When she walks in every guy in the place bites his knuckles and gasps for breath. There are women who just have an acute affect on you. Every time she walks past your knees go so weak you can barely stand. You can hardly breathe. To you she is your Personal Goddess. She is the one. Here's how to get a grip of yourself and her.

Lose the pedestal

With women like this we tend to put them on a pedestal and the longer we go without connecting with her the higher that pedestal gets. You built her up, only you can knock her down – and remember, all your assumptions are only in your head, not hers. She probably hasn't even noticed you yet.

Get real

It's time to stop following her around like a lovesick puppy thinking, 'I'm not worthy, I'm not worthy.' Get real, because she's real. She eats what you eat, breathes the same air, talks the same language, listens to the same music, and yes, she even goes to the toilet. The longer you leave it to make the move, the harder it gets because the more psychological distance you put between yourself and her, the higher she gets up your self-made pedestal.

Get it over with

Forget about all that angst and pain you're torturing yourself with (what if this … what if that …). What's the worst that can happen? She says no. So what? Get over it and move on. She might say yes. Be sure she isn't going to come to you. Women like men who make an effort and work at it.

Talk to her

Instead of setting out to chat her up, start talking to her. Don't rehearse some crappy monologue punctuated with frightening confessions of undying love, and then try and repeat it in front of her. As you cough and splutter and redden, she'll think you a complete basket case and run for the hills. Engage her. Entertain her. Intrigue her. Make her look forward to seeing you. Then, once you've laid the foundations, raise your game.

Never say never

Never pre-guess what a woman's reaction to you will be

People generally are strange creatures, with strange tastes and equally strange motivations for those tastes. And women, like all of us, are often stranger than fiction. They do things for a variety of weird, inexplicable reasons and one of those things can be fancying you.

Read my lips: never ever question why a woman fancies you. This is tantamount to suicide. It's that, 'I couldn't believe she said "yes"' moment.' Don't be so surprised – you're an attractive guy with a lot going for you. Stop being so hard on yourself and start accepting the attention that you are attracting.

When you're in *that* situation where this dynamite babe is practically dripping with desire for you and you can't quite believe it (and I guarantee that this will happen at least once in your life), remove all those doubtful thoughts of 'I can't believe this', 'This can't be happening', or 'What does this incredibly gorgeous woman see in me?'

It could be any one of a zillion irrational reasons: you remind her of her dad, you wear green corduroys and she has a green corduroy fetish, you have a big nose. Who cares? Just wallow in the luxury of her attention.

> **NOTE:** *Once you start questioning her motives you start undermining the process, and if you are stupid enough (and please don't be stupid enough) to convey to her even an inkling of your insecurity – as in 'I can't understand what you see in me' – this smacks of very low self-esteem and she will rapidly get around to asking herself the same question. To which, her answer might be: 'You're right, I must be completely fucking crazy.' And off she jolly well trots.*

I'm not worthy

Here's a cautionary tale. At school at Prince Henry's Grammar School, Otley, there was this girl two years above me. It was one of those situations where I fancied her like mad – I could barely sleep at night – but she was already in the sixth year and was seeing some dork with a sports car (a white Triumph Spitfire to be precise). I couldn't even drive legally. Then one day we found we were working at the weekend at the same hotel and we got on famously. I asked her out and to my surprise she said yes.

Thing was, the asking her out was the easy bit, but what I couldn't get over was the fact that I thought she was too good for me, and I set about subconsciously sabotaging the relationship by not accepting that she might fancy me. I practically shot myself in the foot by repeatedly telling her, or inferring, that she shouldn't be going out with me, and in the end she took my advice and didn't. The relationship self-destructed. I put it all down to the stupidity of youth – I was only fifteen at the time – and chalked it up to experience.

What it taught me, though, was a valuable lesson: never question a woman's motives for finding you attractive. If Charlize Theron walks up to me tomorrow and tells me I am the man of her dreams, and she wants to kiss me all over – she's damn right I am. Let's go.

WORKSHOP 2
Turning a girl 'friend' into a lover (without destroying both relationships)

....

This is that old 'should-I-shouldn't-I' nugget: should I try and leap on my best friend who happens to be a gorgeous hot-bodied babe who I've fancied for ages but haven't done anything about for years on the pretext that I didn't want to ruin a good friend-ship? This, of course is complete bollocks. Why not be honest with yourself and her instead of following her about like a lost sheep in the hope that something somewhere will happen between you. It won't unless you make it happen.

It's one of those student type of scenarios: an 'almost' relation-ship where you both know you want to but neither is keen or brave enough to make the first move, and you end up having endless rounds of burnt toast together into the wee hours of the morning, talking irrelevant rubbish until your mouths get com-pletely dry and your hangovers are developing as you speak.

We all choose people (both men and women friends) who we find attractive in some way, who mirror some part of ourselves. The fact that you spend an inordinate amount of time with this woman, you find her incredibly attractive, wouldn't mind having sex with her and everybody else thinks you're doing it anyway, should tell you something. Look, pal, your right woman is staring you right in the face. Yet you insist on making up excuses why you shouldn't be with her. Duh! Worse, you've probably watched her go through a procession of unsuitable men and heard every confidential graphic detail of why they were completely unsuit-able. What to do? Do this, and hurry because you've probably already wasted about two years of your life.

First, stop and check yourself

You know this woman intimately. All right you've never snogged or slept together, although you've probably seen her naked and spent the odd noble night cuddling each other platonically on a sofa somewhere. Purlease. But you know every other thing about her – what makes her tick, her likes and dislikes, her annoying habits, even the kind of sex she likes; you probably even talk in your own coded language. Blimey, you're practically a married couple.

You have to make the first move

I know you would love it if she ran to you all in a fluster and said, 'I can't go on like this. I've been in love with you since the day we met and I just can't continue as we are, as friends. I love you. I want to shag you within a sinew of your life.' Sorry to shatter your illusion, mate, but it's never going to happen. You have to make the first move. The onus is on you.

Mental preparation

Weigh it up. You can continue as you are, being true friends and not wanting to spoil things but you can get a new best friend anywhere. If you really fancy this woman, then you have to risk losing a friend against the possibility of gaining a lifetime lover who is so perfect for you. Knowing that if she becomes a lover and it works out then this will be a very rewarding relationship since you already know everything about each other. You know that she is your *right woman*. Stop kidding yourself. And the approach here has to be either a) brutal, or b) soft but conniving. But do it when there is no hot hunk on her personal horizon. If there is, wait and let him pass.

Brutal approach

You take her to your favourite bar or coffee bar, maybe after a movie together, so you're both in a good mood (make sure it's a good movie and not depressingly bleak). You can go to a restaurant later if the outcome is favourable.

> **TIP:** *First, order the cappuccinos or drinks, or your waiter will keep bugging you. You sit her down and get all serious. Take a deep breath, take her hand in yours and say something like, 'Janet, I've been thinking about you a lot lately and I've got to tell you that I can't go on being just friends with you. I love being with you. In fact I can't bear being apart from you. I love everything about you and I would really like to take our relationship to a new level.' Here she might try to butt in and say something. Lift your hand gently and nod like a mafia boss to shush her and then continue, 'I understand if you're not interested, but I really am genuinely in love with you and I can't pretend otherwise. We are perfect for each other. What do you think?'*
>
> *Take a slow sip of the cappuccino. If she vomits across the table or starts laughing hysterically take it that you misread the situation. The chances are she will do a mental double take, or repeat what you just said to make sure she heard what you just said, and either a) smile and say 'I thought you'd never ask' and leap across the table and cover you in kisses, the inference being: 'Why did you wait so long?' Or b) she will get all contemplative and analytical and need time to think about it. At this point, don't get drawn into a debate or get defensive and stroppy. Instead, say something like, 'Take your time. Think about it. I'm very serious. Maybe we should get together at the end of the week and see what happens?'*

Soft but conniving

You take her to the bar or coffee bar as before. Settle with the drinks and say, 'Janet. Look, I've got a proposition for you.' At which point she's all ears since she trusts you not to disappoint. 'I've been thinking about us and we can't go on being just good best friends – although I don't want to lose you as a friend. How about we go for a nice weekend away for a 48-hour, no-strings, trial period and if it doesn't work we can revert to being friends again?'

> **TIP:** *Book the hotel before you meet. It shows confidence. And if she blows you out you've no need to mention it.*

You have nothing to lose

If you don't confront the issue, what will happen is she will fall for some completely unsuitable dork and you will lose both a friend and a lover.

5
Women

Know your target market

Women have changed radically in the last twenty years and they are still changing by the minute. They have risen from the ashes of feminism to be smart, sassy, independent, sexy and very capable partners who we should never underestimate or take for granted. They have discovered their sexuality and developed it into a potent force. Yes, they are hugely demanding but they are also very giving, both physically and spiritually, and nine times out of ten they are looking for their *right man* as hard as we are looking for our *right woman*.

The seven ages of women

Women go through many different stages of development and with every new stage come a different set of priorities and level of headspace; and a new attitude to sex, men and relationships. Here are the seven stages that are relevant to you:

1. **Under 16.** Don't even think about it. (See Chapter 10, Be careful out there, page 193)

2. **Age 16–20.** Young, idealistic, brand conscious, fashion conscious, very much into their self and their look, still establishing an image and a persona. They are *hot* and very experimental with sex and different kinds of men, although they will flirt and tease rather than actually do it. They like to feel that they are older than they are and more sexually advanced than they really are. They probably drink more than they can handle and love to exert their sexual power over older men. And display this to their peers.

3. **Age 21–25.** Establishing herself in the world. She's finished school and university and beginning a career. She's very ambitious and idealistic and sexually active. Less brand conscious and more individualistic, she is desperate to forge her own identity and to be seen as her own person as opposed to belonging to a group or tribe. Although now she's face to face with the real world she is beginning to realise how much she doesn't know, which is a rather humbling admission for her to make. This makes her very impressionable and she's therefore very impressed when you take her to a fancy restaurant and show her how to eat escargots or oysters, or take her to a luxury hotel for a night or two away.

4. **Age 26–30.** Getting serious about life, career and relationships. She now considers herself fully grown up and many of her peers will be getting engaged and married, and planning a family. She will be thinking about a serious relationship and long-term, big-ticket items like property and a car, and is getting serious about life, her future and the men in it.

5. **Age 31–35.** Her biological time bomb is ticking furiously and she is seriously broody. She's read the propaganda and knows that 35 is the popular cut-off for having no-risk, healthy children. If she wants to have them then she's looking at men as a potential father, and lifelong partner, not just a one-night stand. Those women uninterested in children will be going at it – working hard and playing hard. I used to know two 30-something committed single women who deliberately went out with the intention of snapping up a different young hunk every night.

6. **Age 36–40.** Children are growing up, her relationship is getting jaded, her routine is uber-boring. Either she's ensconced in a loving, fun relationship with family and good friends, or the relationship has stagnated and entered a downward spiral with everything going pear-shaped. The sex, the fun, the ambition and belief in each other are all going belly-up. She's very susceptible to an affair.

7. **Age 40–50.** Kids are out of the house, husband is out of the way and she's just discovered how attractive she really is. She's willing to take the risks she knows she should have taken earlier in life. A 40-year-old woman with attitude and good looks can be the most potently sexual beast on the planet – witness Michelle Pfeiffer or Elle McPherson.

Most women

Women are complex and trying to second-guess them is a nightmare but there are several elements that cut across women of all ages and backgrounds. Specifically:

- **Most women are not always totally honest.** Many women aren't even honest with themselves, never mind you. They lie to themselves constantly: 'I'll just have one piece of chocolate' before devouring the entire bar; 'I've got nothing to wear' as they open their wardrobe that's bigger than the Oxford Street branch of Marks & Spencer; 'I'm a size ten, really I am' as she tries to squeeze her ample body into a little black dress at least three sizes too small.

- **When a woman says no, she means it, most of the time.** But let's double check shall we? With men they are obtuse and evasive or economical with the truth. The bottom line is they want to keep all their options open. Never trust a woman's first reaction to you. Always go back for a second opinion.

- **Most women don't know what they really want.** A woman is a complex beast and we will never understand her fully. However, it would help if women knew what they wanted, which they don't. Women are completely impulsive – as shoppers, eaters, love-makers and in their choice of men. One minute they fancy an aristocrat in a 1969 Triumph Spitfire, the next a tattooed fairground worker. Trying to second-guess them is impossible. Don't fight it by trying to mould them, use it to your advantage by being their 'other solution'.

- **Most women are incredibly subtle (even when they think they are being blatantly obvious).** Women equate a half-raised eyebrow of interest as the equivalent of a man saying, 'Fancy a shag, love?' Consequently we men generally miss thousands of visual cues of encouragement by not being tuned in to a woman's preferred frequency of micro-communication. It's interesting that other women obviously notice.

Case in point: I once went to a dinner party and gave a girl 'friend' a lift home early. I was surprised when, as soon as we got into the car, she said:

Her: 'I couldn't believe you didn't make a move on Sandra.'

Me: 'Sandra?'

Her: 'Yes, she was flirting outrageously with you all night.'

Me: 'She was?' This was news to me. I had said less than three words to her.

Her: 'She was so obvious, it was embarrassing.'

I dumped her at her flat, thanked her for her insight, and rushed back to the dinner party. She was right.

- **Most women's expectations are totally unrealistic.**
Unfortunately for us, women were brought up on a diet of princess stories where she casts herself as the beautiful heroine and the only men that matter are those very handsome princes who can provide that life-giving, spell-breaking kiss (Snow White), or will save her from domestic drudgery (Cinderella), or climb up her flowing locks and rescue her from solitary confinement (Rapunzel). From the age of two this princess-prince fantasy is already firmly established and for some women this fantasy stays with them to their very lonely grave since their prince, sadly, never arrives. Listen to the lyrics of Marianne Faithful's 'Ballad of Lucy Jordan' – who, at the age of 37 realised she'd never ride through Paris in a sports car with the warm wind in her hair – and you'll get the message. And

know that there are a lot more Lucy Jordans out there than there are Material Girls.

- **Most women expect to 'marry' above themselves.** And will not entertain anyone who is at the same level, or lower, on a long-term basis, although they may dabble with the odd 'bit of rough' along the way.

- **Most women are waiting to be swept into a fantasy.** Although this is changing fast, many women still harbour a real belief that James Bond is going to burn the tyres off his BMW screeching to a halt outside Sainsbury's, before whisking her away from her till point, taking her shopping to Armani, and continuing a Monaco lifestyle together.

- **Most women, once they spiritually commit to you, are incredibly loyal.** The terrific news is: once a woman has decided that, yes, she is keen on you, then you will be over-whelmed by her generosity of body and spirit. Many women have so much love to give and are just waiting for the right opportunity to prove it. There is nothing to compare with connecting with a good woman in terms of their support and overall dedication, yet we constantly take this for granted until it is gone.

> **TIP:** *Never neglect the love of a good woman. Nurture it. Feed it. And once you've found it, thank whatever God you can find.*

The modern older woman

Age is no longer the issue it once was since both men and women seem to be getting younger as they get older. Men look fitter and healthier at 60 than they ever did when they were 40 and women too are holding on to their looks and body shape for longer. It used to be that once a woman hit 40, it was all over and she was resigned to a life of knitting booties and making plum jam. What's exciting about these women today is that not only are they looking terrific and dressing well, but their thinking is modern and out of the box, particularly with regard to sex and relationships. So don't discount the older woman.

How to deal with an older women

The trick with older women is not to insult their age and sense of worldliness. They have been around the block and have their own motivations for choosing a younger man. They may have just come out of a loveless 15-year marriage, their partner could have died or they may just be seeking good sex or a good time. Be sure that they are more adventurous than their peers. And while more patient and forgiving than their younger sisters, they won't stand for crass behaviour, which means you will need to raise your game, clean the flat and stop swearing every second word.

Talk to them with respect

Forget all those clever lines you read in *FHM*. Instead of 'grab your coat, you've scored', try something equally direct but more grown up, like: 'I find you very attractive – can we get together sometime?' If this message is delivered on a note by a waiter to her table with a glass of bubbly, this is a bonus. Older women like men who are, or who at least try to act, gentlemanly.

> **TIP:** *Make sure the waiter is of some calibre and not some snotty student dickhead who will peek at your message, giggle girlishly and pooh-pooh your valour.*

Appreciate that they know more than you

They may not have quite seen it all and done it all but I guarantee that they will have seen and done more than you in most areas. Allow them the space and the opportunity to impart their knowledge, especially in the bedroom. You may be pleasantly shocked to find that she is sexually naïve and looking to experiment. Gently coax her fantasies out of her and indulge them.

Don't make idle boasts

Come clean about what you do and don't know. You will find these women surprisingly forgiving. What? You've never given a woman oral sex? Her ex-husband probably didn't either. Now's your chance to give it a go. Watch her face light up.

Allow her to set the social pace

Older women may be used to a lifestyle that is a few cuts above your normal stomping ground. They are fully aware of this and will certainly ease your burden with their platinum plastic if you're finding the bill at the Ivy somewhat eye-watering.

The modern younger woman

At the other end of the scale women seem to be getting old before their time and maturing at a much younger age. A quick look at teenage magazines like *Sugar*, *More* and *J17* reveals that the topics covered are very sexually explicit indeed

– so much so that Sir Bob Geldof, no less, has been ranting on about what a bad influence they are to teenagers.

This is good and bad. Good, in that women are becoming sexually knowledgeable, if not quite sexually active, earlier, but the bad news is that a 14-year-old can easily dress and look 21 or older. And if you are not vigilant, you can easily find yourself engaging with a minor, which is classed as statutory rape and carries with it a jail sentence. Statutory rape does not look good on your CV. 'But she told me she was twenty-two and worked as a hairdresser' is no defence. A couple of swabs of saliva, a ten-minute DNA match later and your life is over. So be *ultra-careful* out there.

Young girls love experimenting with their power over older men and manufacturing an older 'fantasy' lifestyle, which is probably why men traditionally have always left older women for a younger version of their wife and married slightly lower than their own age. She may look and act like a 25-year-old at 2 a.m. at your friend's party, but you'd be surprised how young she can look in her school uniform, without make-up, in the witness box. Think with your frontal lobe not your frontal probe, especially in the heat of the moment. If you think that a girl looks a trifle too young then she probably is. You can always wait a day or two until you've both sobered up and then check her out more fully.

11 types of women

There are 10 million types of women and every woman is an individual, but here is a selection of the 11 key types that you will meet, what they represent and how to deal with them.

1. The wallflower

Profile. Seemingly unconfident and painfully shy all she needs is a key to unlock all the good stuff that's bottled up inside her. You can be that key.

Her look. Dresses older than she is, often shabby and dowdy, rarely sexy. She needs someone to take her hand, show her the inside of *Vogue* or *Glamour* and take her shopping.

Where to find her? She'll be hiding so you'll need to scour the country and you'll probably only find her by accident: 'Have you met my sister, Candice?' says a friend, at which point the harp music starts and you meet the beautiful wallflower. She will usually be pursuing some lonely, pastoral pursuit like reading. She doesn't often go to parties but when she does look for the 'safe' group at the bottom of the garden, or she'll be talking to a 'safe' man i.e. gay or an older 'mentor' friend. Try bookshops, art galleries, the ballet or classical music recitals.

Why bother? She's a hot woman waiting to happen and she's probably been waiting for years. She's already got a great mind, and she's probably got a great body under those shrouds. If you can get her to bed without scaring her off, you could be in for a big surprise.

The approach. She is a slow burn. The only trick here is to give her your confidence. She will be eternally grateful. Watch her, though – once you've released her from the shackles of inhibition she could go wild, i.e. wilder than you might like.

The downside. She could be past saving.

2. The businesswoman

Profile. She's very hard-working, in control, neat and organised. Inhabits a fast-paced business world and either has her own business or is high up in some corporate giant. She's used to calling the shots and getting her own way and does not suffer fools. She's punctual and very time-conscious.

Her look. Smart and elegant. Sexy, but in a take-your-glasses-off kind of way; she may shock you by dressing completely differently out of her office 'uniform'. So don't be surprised if, when you go to her room to pick her up, she looks like a cowgirl in tassled cowhide jacket and cowgirl boots. Chances are though she will be a smarter or slightly fancier version of what she wore during the day.

Where to find her? Check out hotel bars and restaurants, business conferences and workshops, hospitality tents, the office. You'll probably actually meet her through work at a presentation or sales conference.

The approach. Be straight and to the point. The trick is to divert her away from work. Make it easy for her to say 'Yes' by making her a proposition she can't refuse. Offer to cook her a meal – she has to eat, this gets her to your place and she can relax.

The downside. Her mobile won't stop. Instead of having hot sex at 11.30 p.m. you could be helping her with her Power Point proposal for tomorrow's presentation. As you lie there on her hotel bed twiddling your thumbs in your boxers she'll be sat at the desk in her bra and panties tickling her laptop: 'How do I import the logo from that word document? What's a J-peg? Please help me, darling.' And when she says 'nearly finished' she means another two hours.

The solution. If this is the case let her know that you want to be her lover, not an employee.

3. The yuppie

Profile. A career girl on the move. An alpha-female, she's a professional and could be in the media, finance or the legal professions and is a *Cosmo* gal through and through. She's confident, smart and knows what she wants and is pretty used to getting her own way. She has her *Wallpaper* lifestyle waxed, and her flat is a temple to Philippe Starke, Conran, Jamie Oliver and Martha Stewart. She's also very technologically sussed and a gadget freak. She's the first with the new mobile phone and software.

Her look. Smart and fashionable with a twist. She's trendy but not a fashion victim; she just incorporates what's 'now' into her own look.

Where to find her. Trendy wine bars and the latest hip restaurant or bar she read about in *Tatler* or *Glamour*. Shopping at select stores only, she wouldn't be seen dead at Marks & Spencer.

The approach. Show her your new iPod.

The downside. She meets plenty of other men who are attractive, wealthy and powerful.

4. The hippy-trippy

Profile. Stuck in a time warp, she embraces all the original hippy values of love and peace, plays the mandolin and the penny flute, listens to old vinyl copies of Yes and

Tyrannosaurus Rex, and smokes dope. She's a confirmed vegetarian, very nurturing and caring, and surprisingly family orientated, although she'll probably call her daughter something whacky like Moon Shadow.

Where to find her. Glastonbury, folk clubs, Camden Market, dope shops and anywhere where they sell beads, candles and rolls of purple velvet.

Her look. Either flea-market shabby or, if she's reasonably well off, a shabby-chic Hermes hippy. She's swathed in folds of purple and green velvet, and floral prints complete with nose ring, clogs and hundreds of bangles and rings, each with its own meaning.

The approach. You really need to share the dream and be plugged into her network. She's never going to step into a 5-series BMW for oysters at Claridges. You need to be excited by star signs and deep ethereal and spiritual philosophies. Offer her a joint or a clever way of marketing her beaded knick-knacks.

The upside. Surprisingly good at sex and very experimental, although tends to dwell on some faddish element like Tantric sex. 'I knew a guy once who didn't ejaculate for twelve years,' she'll announce proudly, out of the blue. (His balls must have been the same colour and size of watermelons!)

The downside. Might live or aspire to living in a wigwam. Do you want to listen to Tyrannosaurus Rex and Yes albums? I don't know about you, but when I have sex I *like* to ejaculate.

5. The Essex girl

Profile. Essex girl is the UK shorthand for every shop girl and receptionist in the country. Young, attractive, usually busty, always with great legs, she's smiley, fun and confident in a very street-smart way. She's the salt of the earth, the girl next door and all the other clichés rolled into one. These girls like sex. They're not rocket scientists and will never win *The Weakest Link* and they know it. Sex is what they do well. Brought up on a diet of Page 3, and hot pop tottie they've seen what 'sexy' has done for the Spice Girls, Atomic Kitten and an army of Page 3 girls. These are her role models. Basically she would kill to leave her job on the make-up counter at Boots to announce the footy news on Sky TV and then be on the cover of *FHM* in a wet T-shirt.

The look. Squeezed into tight jeans or a short skirt and tight top with something daring or revealing to show off her best assets. Court shoes with a high heel.

Where to find her? Usually at the till point. Essex girls will get completely pissed with the 'gals' at theme restaurants and bars before moving on to scope the lads at key nightclubs. On holiday you will find marauding droves of them hopping from bar to bar.

The approach. Laddish. Cheeky chappie. Macho. Flash. Helps if you're a Premier League footballer.

The downside. There are only 220 first-team Premier League footballers. Are you one?

6. The intellectual/academic

Profile. Intense, earnest, and a tad too serious, she is the student who never grew up. She listens to Mozart, goes to the opera and always throws in a quote from some intellectual into any conversation. 'As Dante said: "blah blah blah".' Probably has family money or a trust fund that supports her 'Bohemian' or 'philanthropic' lifestyle.

Where to find her. She'll always be near a campus of some sort and will be affiliated in some way to the university lifestyle for the rest of her life.

The look. Out of touch with trends, but not badly dressed, she still needs a serious make-over before showing her off.

The approach. You've either got to join her club and be equally as academic as she is – or the total opposite and take her out of herself. Why is she an academic? Why does she choose to stay at school when most other people can't wait to get shot of the place? Up to now her life has been all theory; put some of it into practice. Show her the outside of a lecture hall and she will probably blossom into a sex goddess overnight.

The downside. Her friends from university are pretty dull and boring.

7. The international traveller

Profile. She travels light and knows her way around six European capitals and might have property in one or two of them (you hope). Fluent in two or three languages.

The look. Dressed head to toe in duty-free luxury labels, the watch, the scarf, the luggage – Hermes, Louis Vuitton, Pierre Cardin, Chanel. She's tanned and worldly with a confident but friendly air. Calm and used to dealing with situations, she will give the benefit of the doubt.

Where to find her. Airport transit lounges.

The approach. If she's got the time and the inclination she's pretty open to company and given her tight fly-in, fly-out schedule she will realise the urgency of the situation. If she likes you, you could find yourself in her hotel room or pied-à-terre quicker than you thought humanly possible. Après sex will be short-lived and then she will be off again.

Why bother? This could develop into an interesting and rewarding little sexual sideline if every time she pops into the country she leaps on your bones for a hectic sex session. It's your mutual little secret (but don't fall in love with her before reading Taming the female 'Romeo', page 162).

8. The victim

Profile. Drama queen deluxe. Everything is a mission. Every time you pick up the phone something has gone wrong in her life. Her car broke down, she twisted her wrist falling off a bar stool, she's been burged six times in a month ... the woman is a disaster area. Eventually you get to the point where you don't want to ring her or when you do, you simply ask, what now?

The look. This can be any kind of woman.

Where to find her. Casualty ward – this woman is everywhere.

The approach. She needs saving from herself, so save her. Once you get over the fixing and patching up there is a woman crying out for help or attention. Give her some. Once you've rehabilitated her and gained her trust she will stop with the disaster routine.

The downside. Saving her from herself or fixing something of hers that she's broken is a full-time job.

9. The single mum

Profile. Unless she, or her ex, is loaded and generous, single mums have a huge disadvantage with regard to time, money, availability and eligibility. They are invariably struggling to keep everything together and make ends meet. They get tired and disenchanted easily and are fed up with putting on a brave face to the world. Although they love their child/ren they are bored stiff with kids' company and other doting mothers, and crave adult conversation and a grown-up to give them some love and affection. Also, they wouldn't say no to some quality sex. Single mums are either in the relegation zone, or have dropped out of the Premier League and they know it.

Where to find her. Tesco's or Sainsbury's with trolleys bursting with Coco-Pops, gimmicky yoghurts and microwaveable dinners.

The approach. Just get to know her and get her to trust you. Let her know that you know how tough it is in a subtle way without her thinking she's a charity fuck. Give her solutions not problems and work around her. Make it easier for her to say yes by helping her better organise her time or, if you can afford it, hiring a baby-sitter. Treat her to the things she's been missing – restaurants, movies, concerts, life.

Why bother? Given that over a third of marriages end in tears, many of them with children involved, then there are a hell of a lot of fantastic, sexy women stuck in a world of domestic drudgery just waiting to be rescued. Throw her a lifeline and you will be rewarded tenfold. You could keep it as a regular ongoing 'affair'. Or, if you are keen on settling down, it's a way of gaining an instant ready-made family and trying out family life. At least you get to road-test the kids before moving in. You can bring enormous warmth and hope to what was a 'dysfunctional' family situation and you can completely revolutionise a single mum's life if you have the will. In return, she will love you for ever.

The downside. She will always have a child and an ex. The child will either get on with you famously or will make your life hell. Believe me, if the ex irritated her then he sure as hell will irritate you.

> **TIP:** *Choose a woman with children over two – you'll avoid the nappy and puking stages; and it might help if she is young enough to have one of your own, if you're up for it.*

10. The divorced woman

Profile. Divorced women fall roughly into two broad categories: 1) those who are miserable, bitter, depressed, grief-stricken, basket cases and generally hostile towards men; and 2) those who couldn't wait to break free – they're adventurous, strong and fun, and so want to catch up on everything they've been missing. Consequently they are willing to try almost anything (including you), and without the need to justify their actions to anyone else they are a gift which you should accept gracefully.

> **TIP:** *Aim for Type 2.*

Divorced women certainly have learnt a lesson or two so the chances are that they certainly know what they do and do not want in a man, and they will be aiming to avoid making the same mistake twice. She will usually go through a period of sexual experimentation during which she enjoys her new-found freedom – leaping on a variety of men – but will eventually want to settle down to a steady relationship again. If a divorced woman chooses you for a long-term partner, then you can be 90 per cent sure that this is not a light decision and you must have what she's looking for.

11. Widows

This is an interesting one since we all tend to think of widows as being 80-year-old bats whose lifetime husband has just passed away and they won't be long in following. Yet there are thousands of young attractive guys dying every day, leaving even younger, more attractive wives who (providing he did the right thing by insuring his life properly and making a will) suddenly find the house and car paid for and have a house full of his stuff. And once the grief has abated, they enter a new exciting phase of their life when they discover that there is a big world out there that needs to be explored, and they suddenly need help with the exploring.

There are a couple of choice rules for widows:

1. Get them away from close friends who will persist in making them feel guilty for talking to anyone other than their dead husband. It's amazing how their 'good' friends will want to control them and keep them locked into this cycle of grief much longer than they

would have stayed there. Suggest a 'no pressure' holiday to get away from it all. She won't mind chipping in half.

2. Get them away from the family seat. Remove her geographically from the scene of the grief, albeit temporarily. She needs to get over it, move on and make a fresh start, and you can help her with that.

Sitting ducks – women as a captive audience

There is a set of women who work in an environment where they are paid to serve you with a smile. This includes waitresses, bar-women, air stewardesses, rent-a-car and hotel staff among others, but the common denominator is that the woman is at your beck and call and she is generally friendly and welcoming, attentive and caring.

Given such a scenario, if the woman is also attractive – bonus points – we suddenly have a situation that *seems* as though this is a falling-off-a-log experience. I mean, you didn't even have to go anywhere or spend any money to meet her (except the meal or car hire, of course). Be warned: being in the service/ hospitality industry means that smiling and friendliness are part of the stock-in-trade so do not take these personally. She does this to everyone. Now if you do fancy the waitress or the hotel receptionist you've got several initial problems to overcome:

• Whatever you say and do, she will have heard it at least nine million times before and while you are meeting her for the very first time, she meets a new one of you every minute of her life.

• Behind that sweet smile, she is cynical, bored, frustrated and badly paid; she's sick of men hitting on her and is trying to work out how much of a tip you're going to leave. Therefore she would seem not that great a prospect.

- She's probably not even allowed to fraternise with 'guests' or clients by order of the management. So she couldn't even if she wanted to.

So now what?

I've found with service or hospitality staff that there are a few choice rules of engagement that will get her on your side, if not quite into bed (yet):

- First, realise that discretion is king and you will need to respect her position and the environment in which she works. Hotels particularly have rigid rules and a weird, almost medieval hierarchy of power.

- Ask her what her name is, or check out her name badge and use it frequently.

- Be polite and deliberately say please and thank you a lot. (This will be music to her ears since they very rarely get treated like anything other than slaves by the masses.)

- If you can't contain your excitement and feel the need to say something like 'Fuck me, she's a bit of all right' to your mates, don't let her hear it. And don't come out with, or let your tactless cretin of a colleague come out with, anything crass or embarrassing like 'We're bra designers – are you a 36b or c?' She will hate you both and probably spit in your cappuccinos. Rightly so.

- Try and get some modicum of conversation out of her –

any kind of interaction will do. If you can find out what she does when she's not working or where she hangs out, bonus.

- If you want to speak to her away from your mate/s or your colleague/s, when you are finished, leave your car keys on the table/counter and then when everyone is outside, go back in for them.

- Arrange to meet her. Get her telephone number. The good thing is, she isn't really going anywhere; you know where she is and can revisit on your own in your own time, so don't rush it. If you're staying at a hotel ask her, 'Will you be here when we get back at 4 p.m.?' and then lead in to what her plans are for the evening.

> **TIP:** *If you do make a date, she won't want to sit in the hotel restaurant where she works and have all the staff pointing and gawking at her. Do something imaginative.*

Danger – women at work

There are some women who, despite their initial attractiveness, you need to be aware of and avoid like the plague.

The gold-digger
There are an enormous amount of very wealthy guys out there and this fact has not escaped a certain type of woman who hungers for the good life at any price. Which is why, if you wander down the quays of playboy theme parks like Atlantis on Paradise Island, Bahamas, Tortilla in the British Virgin Islands, Marbella or Monaco, you will see a fleet of short, fat, balding business tycoons on 60-foot yachts surrounded by

tanned, big-breasted, long-legged, bikini-clad 'beauties'. That's right, gold-diggers.

Look, if you've got minus 60 quid in your NatWest current account, are two months behind on your mortgage and American Express have trained snipers camped out in the tree opposite your flat, you should have no worries. This woman will take one surreptitious look at your bank statements (while you've nipped down the road to fetch the paper and milk and thought she was still sleeping!) and she'll be out of your life like a bat out of hell.

However, if you do have a certain moneyed portfolio, trust funds coming out of your ears and your family have banked at Coutts for six generations, be careful. Be very careful. A practised gold-digger can haemorrhage money a hundred times faster than you can make it.

The psycho

Sometimes you come across a woman who just doesn't add up. She's attractive and personable but there's something quite deranged about her which you can't quite put your finger on. I'll tell you why – she is a complete nutter. Underestimate this woman at your peril, because she is seriously dangerous and destructive and can wreak havoc with your mind, ruin your career and make your life absolute hell. You must have noted the Glen Close character in *Fatal Attraction*, the one who boils Michael Douglas's rabbit? Well, you need to spot a bunny-boiler long before she pots your long-eared friend. These women will try to possess you, so watch for the warning signs. These tell-tale patterns should set the alarm bells ringing.

Marks of ownership

She's the sort of woman who will claw your back viciously with her long sharp nails, leaving unsightly red weals and raw wounds as a mark of her 'ownership' of you. And despite your asking her not to give you love bites she insists on biting you in a very visible spot, leaving an ugly bruise for everyone to see. This is her way of leaving her brand and marking her territory. It says: you are hers, hands off.

Obsessive behaviour

She flies into a blind rage when you say you have to go to an office or client dinner without her, or need to fly to Paris for a two-day conference, even though wives and partners aren't invited. She wants you to herself 24 hours a day and she will go to increasing lengths to keep you there. Strange things will begin to happen. You will kiss her goodbye after a terrific night, go downstairs and then be unable to find your car keys, although you know you always keep them in your right-hand jacket pocket. After you spend hours looking for them, and are getting serious sense-of-humour failure, she will suddenly dip her hand behind the couch and, hey presto! announce, 'Here they are.' At a later stage, when she progresses to a more desperate level, you may find your tyre slashed or the valve taken out.

Unwarranted jealousy

You make an innocent remark about a passing woman – 'Aren't her shoes fabulous?' – and suddenly find yourself in a combat zone: the psycho will turn on you and almost slap your face. And should you ever spend time with another woman – attractive or not – for any reason whatsoever, she will go ballistic.

Begins to interfere in every aspect of your life

You mention that Jenkins at work is driving you mad and putting unnecessary pressure on you with his demands for sales figures and presentations. Next minute Jenkins starts getting obscene phone calls or e-mails and your name is 'accidentally' mentioned. Either that or, when she's angry with you, she starts making mischief by calling up your boss and asking him if he knew you were gay or that you had Aids.

The professional 'serial' dater

There are some women who simply love to go on dates and that's it. They will actively flirt with and date lots (and lots, and lots) of men but never put out to any of them and think it all perfectly normal. She might innocently even tell you all about her other 'men' and how excited she is about them. She just loves the attention of having men drool over her and spend money on her, but is the celebrated queen of cock-teasers. She's a 'serial' dater. If you ever get inside her flat (you'd probably have to break in) it would look like a church harvest festival where grown men worship at her altar: long-stemmed roses from Nigel, St Joseph's lilies from Steven, chocolates from Peter, theatre tickets from Rupert. You can go out with her for weeks and you won't get any further than holding hands and a peck on the cheek, if that. Yes, she looks great and dresses well, says all the right things, makes the right moves and seems or claims to be keen on you – but nothing ever happens. She is probably still a virgin even if she is 28 years old.

These professional daters are quite clever in that they seem to have an uncanny charm and a peculiar knack of disarming your testosterone. You feel strange around them, like you're a cuddly toy and they've taken your batteries out. They'll reel you in and then let you go like the horny old trout you are. You are her plaything and completely under her spell.

Is it just you?

No, don't worry, she does it to *everyone*. The trick here is to force her hand and put her on the spot. After your third date, when you escort her to the doorstep of her flat, instead of shuffling away in your usual semi-apologetic manner, move in for a sloppy wet kiss on the lips. If she is shocked and horrified, screams and tries to avoid your kiss with the same desperation as a cat trying to avoid a bucket of water, you have your answer. Avoid any temptation to force yourself on her either physically or verbally, as in 'Come on, you know you want it.' This is entering very dangerous territory and is called date rape (see Chapter 10, Be careful out there, page 193). You could try discussing it with her, but I wouldn't recommend it – you'd just spend all night on the step talking in ever-decreasing circles. I suggest you get out while you're ahead. She's a lost cause. Let some other poor sap waste his time and money chasing her around. You need to know when to call it a day.

WORKSHOP 3
Work the party like a pro
•• ••••••••••••••••••

Make women fall at your feet, without tripping them up

Most guys are lazy. They want it delivered on a plate without putting in any effort. At a party they'll stand by the bar, swilling the lagers and guzzling the nuts until about half an hour from the end of the party and then think, 'Jeez, I better go and chat somebody up.' Fuelled with Dutch courage they'll make a few clumsy attempts at bowling a maiden over and then, embarrassed, they'll chase down a few tequilas, saunter home and masturbate themselves to sleep. Next morning they wake up thinking they had a great time. If this sounds frighteningly familiar or sounds like something you wish to avoid, read on before the guests arrive.

The party is a great equaliser and women reward men who put

in the time and the effort. So if you plan on standing in the kitchen burping your way through a dozen Amstels and a bucket of finger food, do this instead.

The early worm gets the bird

Avoid the temptation to arrive fashionably late, which in London is half an hour and in Edinburgh is about an hour and a half. Arrive at the party early. Why? People are very vulnerable before everybody arrives and the party gets going. They don't know anybody, nobody is talking to anyone else and any cliques that exist already split the room. Consequently women are welcoming and eager to chat. Target somebody early and go up and introduce yourself. Be confident, casual, polite and especially friendly (but not familiar). Offer to get her a drink. Your confidence will be noted.

Be chatty without chatting her up. Forget clever lines like 'get your coat you've scored' and save your what-do-you-do, who-do-you-know spiel for a little later. Talk about something innocent and arbitrary. Think of her as a friend of your mum's, or your sister-in-law. Make simple open-ended conversation that she can respond to without a yes or no answer. 'What do you think of the painting?' or 'The food looks amazing — what do you think? Do you like prawns?' The more ordinary and non-threatening the conversation, the easier and more comforting it is for her. Be warned, though, only losers say things like 'Nobody talking to you, either?' At the moment you're just an interesting, charming gentleman without any obvious downside. Don't reveal too much about yourself. Let her do the talking and gently nudge her along. Stay there for a while, watch the room fill, and then . . .

Leave her wanting more

Make an excuse and move away. Say, 'Excuse me a minute — I

must just talk to so and so,' and disappear. Just before you leave her side, compliment her on something. Don't make a big deal out of it, just a simple 'Nice talking to you', and By the way, your hair looks fabulous.'

As you disappear, she'll think you're in demand, which instils a willingness to compete. She'll be curious as a dog. which means she'll ask somebody else about you, which in turn will make you sound even more interesting.

Remember this: you can never know enough women because women lead to other women. If her drop-dead gorgeous mate arrives she'll enthuse about you to her, and there is no better introduction than a recommendation from another woman.

Repeat yourself

Then go and do the exact same thing to another woman across the room. She'll think you know the other one. And vice versa. This is the process of 'engaging' by which you create demand for yourself. Ignore your mates getting pissed at the bar and leering at the hostess. And don't tell them what you're doing or how you're doing at any stage throughout the party, otherwise they will pooh-pooh your initiative and immediately try and sabotage your efforts.

Depending on the size and the layout of the party you could probably 'engage' three, four, even five times at a decent bash. Concentrate on the women. Don't get stuck with Jenkins who you know vaguely from work and who wants to bore you about budget cuts for the new fiscal year. You're on a mission.

Once you've completed your first circuit, ease off. Go and have a breather and check on your mates. Resist the urge to get excited and boast, 'I think I'm in with that blonde in the purple dress.' Give it fifteen minutes, check to see who's arriving, charge your glass and then steel yourself for more.

The second wave

Start again. Single out the first woman you spoke to and bump into her again. This isn't difficult. A nice touch is to take her a drink. If she's talking to someone else — male or female — don't panic, simply join the group as naturally as possible. Offer her the drink and say you thought she might need some sustenance. If she's talking to a guy, gauge the competition, and if it's a woman, introduce yourself. Then focus on your 'friend'.

Once you've been accepted into the group you can quickly isolate her. She will be less vulnerable having found her comfort zone and the alcohol should be taking effect, making her less inhibited. Don't be surprised if she's pleased to see you and grabs your arm or makes some other physical gesture. The music will have been turned up a notch and you can lean closer to her, which makes it all the more intimate. Touch her gently on the arm when talking. Put your arm on her back to protect her when some guys jostle past with a handful of beers, but no funny stuff. Don't try and stick your tongue down her throat the moment she leans closer to you.

Now you can afford to be a little cheeky and tease her. Say something along the lines of, 'I thought you were avoiding me', or fondle her wrap and say, 'Your pashmina looks much better on you than on the goat.' Know the difference between cheek and insulting. She should give as good as she gets, which warms the conversation, peppers it with humour and takes it to a more familiar level. This is the time to get more personal and check on her availability. Wait for a natural break — if the conversation plateaus, or her friend interrupts, then off you go again. Smile and wave and say, 'I'll be back in a minute' — unless of course you've already made up your mind.

By the time you've completed your second round, you will have a pretty good idea of who is interested and who isn't. Again, take a breather and compose yourself. Drink just enough to catch a buzz but watch it. If you start slurring your words, you're history.

The third wave

By now the party is seriously cooking. The drink has taken its effect, the music is loud and everyone is suitably warmed up. It's time to make up your mind if you haven't already. When you go back to your chosen prospect you're now so familiar it's like you've known each other for years. If she has been cornered by some tall, dashing merchant banker, don't give up without first checking. It may be her brother-in-law.

You can sneakily force her hand by teasing her with, 'I'd better leave you to it – don't want to cramp your style', while nodding at the prospective guy. She will reply very sincerely. No, we're just good friends. Maybe even grab your arm and say, no, don't go. Let her do the physical stuff – she'll let you know when she's ready.

Bingo

You're getting on famously, so don't now throw it all away. The trick is to get her away from the party as soon as possible. Suggest that you go for a nightcap or a cappuccino somewhere else. Maybe even a simple walk in the garden.

Be honest about your intentions. You want to get her on her own and talk to her somewhere quiet. At this stage, bear this in mind: you don't have to sleep with her tonight. Why put that pressure on yourself? Once you accept that, then you will be more natural and the pressure will ease. She will like you for it and respond. Of course, if you get in the car and she's all over you like a rash, then head for home, or the summerhouse, immediately. The rest is up to you.

Don't force it, though

Avoid the temptation to take her home that night, and don't get all sulky and stub your toes in the gravel if she doesn't want to. Give her room. See her to her car, even drive her home. Make an arrangement for another evening. You can always go back to the party.

Save her

Keep your eyes on her and beware of people movements. If she gets caught with the village bore, go and rescue her. It's the modern equivalent of fighting the dragon. Just step up, grab her arm and say, 'Jennifer, there's somebody I need you to meet' – it happens at parties all the time – 'Sorry', and whisk her off. Don't make an issue out of it or give the bore time to react. Smile. Then say to her, 'Sorry about that, I wanted to get you alone.' She will be thankful.

6
Communication

Forget all the implications and ramifications, dynamics and undercurrents – don't analyse what you are saying, just talk.

Talking to women

We live in one of the most literate societies in the world. We consume rainforests of reading matter on a daily basis and there is no shortage of hot topics to talk about and voice an opinion on. Yet when it comes to talking to women, particularly your *right woman*, we tend to turn into an inept preschooler as our saliva glands dry up and our tongues get stuck to the roof of our mouths. This need not be so

It's interesting how we throw obstacles in our own way. We see the act of talking to a woman as a battle which we've turned into a life-and-death, us-and-them, shit-or-bust situation and we pile the stakes so high that we've made it far too complicated for ourselves, setting ourselves up for rejection. The other thing is: we tend to forget to have fun and make it fun for the other person.

There's a tendency for us to skirt around issues we really want to talk about in a vain attempt to try and convey to her that you're not really trying to chat her up. With our language and body language we're subconsciously saying, 'I know it looks like I'm chatting you up but I'm not really chatting you up. I mean, I don't really want to shag you – we're just talking, aren't we?' Problem here is that a) you're tying yourself up in unnecessary knots, b) you are coming across as incredibly wet, and c) she might actually want you to shag her. Look, forget all the implications and ramifications, dynamics and undercurrents – don't analyse what you are doing, just talk.

19 hot opening gambits

Just like you play your best round of golf when it doesn't matter, the act of engaging with a woman is easiest when the consequences don't matter. When it does, that's when the bogeyman appears. Just try to think of the woman you are talking to as a favourite old aunt and don't be afraid of saying normal, mundane stuff that is shallow and meaningless.

I used to do loads of interviews with celebrities for magazines, and spent hours and hours transcribing the tape-recordings – most of what was said was complete crap. It was only when I distilled a one-hour tape into a 2,000-word written interview that it made any sense. If you analyse any conversation – for instance, if you tape-recorded your average dinner party – you would find that people from every walk of life and level of intelligence talk utter drivel. Especially after six bottles of Jacob's Creek. Not much of our day-to-day talk is mind-blowingly riveting, yet when we 'talk to a woman, we make a rod for our back by expecting ourselves to come out with something highly profound, something that has the wisdom of Dante and wit of Shakespeare rolled into one. Don't be so hard on yourself. Just chat normally.

And avoid those tired old one-liners: 'Cheer up, love, it might never happen', 'Get your coat, love, you've scored', 'Sit on my face and I'll guess your weight', and other macho missives. Asking the time and for directions is considered weak, and that haven't-I-seen-you-somewhere-before approach – 'I'm sure I know you', when she doesn't know you from Adam – is cringingly embarrassing. Some men believe that the best approach is a lack of approach, based on the Buddhist theory that the less you do the more you get, but this smacks of laziness and if even if you do look like Keanu Reeves, you still need to put in the groundwork.

The basics

1. **Keep introductions simple.** Say, 'Hi, I'm Mike, what's your name?' while offering your hand. Don't complicate matters. Do this and a) you're already touching her, b) she has to respond, and c) you now know her name and she knows yours. Not a bad start. The fact that you approached her with such a positive manner exudes confidence. She'll like that.

    Remember, you don't have to explain your motives or justify why you're talking to her.

2. **Establish her background.** Why is she where she is – who does she know at the party, what company is she

with at the exhibition or which department at the conference? It's become terribly unfashionable to ask people
what they do, but there's no getting away from it, what
we do defines who we are, and the quicker we know
what somebody is, the more rapidly we can piece
together their profile and whether or not it coincides
with what we're looking for. If so, let's move to the next
round. If not, delete and move on.

3. **Don't be afraid to tease her.** When someone introduces
   you with 'This is Pamela, she's—', smile and interrupt
   while taking her hand. 'Don't tell me, I bet you're a–'
   pause for effect '–vet, hairdresser, lingerie designer, photographer.' This allows you to place her under the spot-
   light and flatter her. She'll want to know how you came
   to your assessment and will have to ask why you
   thought that.
       'Oh you have that air of confidence, that knowing
   look' or 'You just look very creative' – whatever, you can
   now wax lyrical to your heart's content. She immediately knows what you think of her, you're in the thick of a
   conversation and you command 110 per cent of her
   interest. That's exactly where you want to be.

   Note: She will probably be something completely different. In which case you can add a bit of self-deprecation:
   'It doesn't surprise me – I always was a bad judge of
   character.' Or 'Well, that's even more interesting.' Now
   you're styling. Why? This allows you to throw in all sorts
   of positive assessments and statements, and thinly disguised compliments.

4. **Enforced familiarity.** You can catch a woman out and
   have her talking before she knows it if you catch her off

guard. Choose something neutral and feasible. At the office:

You: 'Are you Suzy from the Research Department, who's working on the Manhattan Project?'

Her (taken aback): 'No, certainly not.'

You: 'Well, who the bloody hell are you then and what have you done with Suzy?'

5. **Challenge her.** Women love to be challenged and many women can't stand losing, which are two qualities you should easily be taking advantage of. For example, you go up to a woman and in the course of conversation say, 'Are you a spontaneous kind of woman?' There are few women who would like to admit that they aren't, even if they are actually timid little mice. They are hardly likely to say, 'No, I'm a boring old fart and haven't an ounce of adventure in me.' So you're on a safe wicket that she will say, 'Of course.' Moving along, the next issue is 'But how spontaneous are you – moderately, very or extremely?'

Once you've ascertained that she is to some degree spontaneous, then you can push her to be spontaneous with you. This works because she's already committed herself to being spontaneous, whether or not it's with you, so if you offer her a nice challenge – whether it's to go skinny-dipping in the lake, fly with you to Paris for the weekend or visit the local sex club together – she's already psychologically painted herself into a corner and is more likely to say 'yes'.

Even if she backs out of flying to Paris or the sex club, you can scale down and soften the challenge by saying, 'OK then, let's settle for a nightcap at the hotel bar.' The fact that you've offered her a manageable escape will be doubly appreciated.

> **TIP:** *Make sure the challenge you set her is in keeping with her style, her social standing and your joint circumstance, i.e. to go skinny-dipping in a lake, you need to be near a lake.*

6. **Be blunt.** We've all heard the urban legends about guys who just go up to as many women as they can find and say, 'Wanna fuck?' until they find somebody who says yes. Well there's blunt and there's blunt. Rather let your intentions be known from the start but in a more dynamic and socially acceptable way. The socially accepted version of 'Do you wanna fuck?' is 'Can I kiss you later?'

   A more seasoned approach is to walk up to her positively and say, 'You look interesting; what's your story?' Resist the temptation to be so blunt that you say, 'You look gorgeous' or put the focus on one obvious body part – 'Your legs are sensational.' First of all she will see your being impressed by her looks as shallow, and she's probably used to it to the point of being heavily bored by it. Slip your compliments in later when you've got her talking.

7. **Defence mechanism.** 'I hate women like you' will put her on the defensive but seriously spike her interest. Nobody likes to be disliked, never mind hated. You have to say it shaking your head with a half-smile otherwise you will really upset her.

   Her (slightly flustered): 'Why, what do you mean? We've only just met.'

You: 'Because you're just far too perfect You'd bring out the worst in me.'

Her relief will visibly wash over her. She has turned what she thought was an enemy into a friend. You now need to use that advantage point and turn her from a new friend into a lover.

Unorthodox but powerful

8. **Creating a sense of urgency.** There's nothing like a hit-and-run moment for leaving a woman in a breathless whirl and wanting more. Use this shock technique and you'll create a real stir that will make you immediately enigmatic. It doesn't matter where you are or how much time you've really got, pretend you're in a real rush.

   Try striding straight up to a woman and, using your own words, say something like, 'Sorry to bother you but I've been watching you for the past five minutes and you look like the most interesting/sexy/desirable woman I've ever seen.' Before she can respond, carry on talking. 'I know this is a little unusual, but I'm in a terrible hurry to catch a train/plane/ferry (or to make a meeting).' Stick your business card in her hand and carry on. 'I'd love to meet you for a drink. Please call me if only to say "thanks but no thanks".' Before you go, grip her by her arms or hand (do not brush her breasts) and say something like 'You ... are ... gorgeous' in this emphatic, staccato way. Then run off into the crowds like the scared bunny rabbit you feel.

   I guarantee that this will have never happened to her before. She will talk about this for weeks and be flattered as hell. The first thing she will do when she gets to the office is tell her best mate and confidante who won't believe her, but then become as curious as hell and inspect your business card (make sure it's reasonably impressive, i.e. not Organic Effluent Distributor). She will be dying to know more and will egg on your girl to call you up and progress the relationship. You can just hear them: 'Oh go on, you've got nothing to lose.' She will drive your girl nuts and will pester her to death. 'Have you called him yet?'

She may not ring within 48 hours but she *will* ring. When she does, be all relieved to hear from her and semi-apologetic. 'I'm so glad you called. I thought I must have put you off with my shock tactics or you weren't interested.'

9. **Dream sequence – 'I had a dream about you last night'.**
   This is one of the most underrated approaches a man can make, yet I've used this many times and been utterly surprised at how you can capture a woman's interest by this one simple phrase. It's powerful and works because of a combination of intrigue and the unknown, and the special focus on her – I mean, you dreamt about her last night; that's really something. Watch her eyes light up and get all mischievous or flushed as she feels completely singled out and special. Women love this kind of thing.

   The next obvious question is, what, particularly, did you dream about her last night, i.e. what happened? What was she doing in your dream? Here your imagination is your only limit, but the delivery is the carrot that keeps her interest. It works best with somebody you have seen around a couple of times, and chatted to, although you might not be going out with them. If you can add, 'I'll tell you about it later' as you disappear, this will have her thinking about you for hours.

When you do tell her; you have to keep the suspense going and turn it into a flirtatious game of intrigue. The major thing is that you don't want to built it up to a deafening crescendo and follow that with an anti-climax, such as she did something very ordinary like had some supporting role pushing a supermarket trolley and buying grapefruit. And you can't be so crass as to turn her right off, right away, as in 'You were giving me a blow job and I came between your tits. You were fantastic.'

Here, it isn't the graphic detail; it's the idea that's romantic and intriguing, so talk in broad strokes. You have to spin it out and it's a good vehicle for inad-vertently complimenting her along the way, weaving an ego-booster into the story as in 'You looked fan-tastic and incredibly sexy, which you do most of the time anyway, and then ...' this happened and that happened.

She's always going to be expecting something vaguely sexual in the dream, whether she's up for it or not in real life. So don't disappoint her. But tease her, and offer some amateur psychological analysis along the way: 'This obviously means that you are an incredibly sexy and ... woman.' It isn't really the dream, it's the telling of the dream that a) gives you her undivided attention, b) allows you to compliment her and let her know how you feel about her, and c) allows you to elaborate on a clever but thinly disguised come-on.

If she presses you for erotic detail say, 'I couldn't pos-sibly go into detail – I hardly know you. Suffice to say that you were everything I've dreamt about and more.'

10. **Fun and cheeky.** You need to grab the moment whenever even half an opportunity presents itself.

    So you see a great-looking woman behind the counter in a boutique or standing at a bar, just stick your head around the door and say, 'Just checking – have you got a boyfriend at the moment?'

    She shakes her head. 'Not at the moment.'

    You say, 'Do you want one? Like tonight?'

    This is a very off-the-cuff approach but is sure to raise a smile even if you don't get anywhere. Those who don't ask, don't get. If she says, sorry I'm married, or I've already got a boyfriend, say something like, 'That is so depressing. Have you got a sister?' At least you will have made her smile.

    (My personal best happened as I was once walking down the street slightly behind this hard-bodied babe, when a couple of builders started whistling and making comments at her. I quickened my step and as she looked across at me I said to her, 'I'm so sick of builders whistling at me – they do it all the time', at which point she couldn't help but smile.)

Moving things along

Once you've broken the ice you need to move the conversation along to a new level to keep her interest going and find that all-important common ground.

11. **Find the common denominator.** The quicker you find out something about her that you can connect with, the better. It doesn't matter whether it's Renaissance painting, skydiving, pets, household herbs or cars, or the fact that you both holidayed in Wales as a child, you need to probe her until you find the one thing that unites you. I once met this Swedish girl on a train from Amsterdam

to Athens. She was friendly but cool and I thought 'no chance'. We talked politely for ages but it was only when we discovered that we had both learnt Russian at school (and forgotten most of it) that she thawed out and became unbelievably animated. We spent hours remembering various words and phrases, writing the letters of the Cyrillic alphabet on the steamy carriage windows. That night we shared a terrific evening together in our private carriage and made love as the train sped through Trieste.

12. **Talk about her.** We all like talking about ourselves because it's what we know best. Women are no exception and they feel very comfortable talking about themselves. Chip away with open-ended questions and she should keep going for ever, but don't allow her to ramble. Keep pointing her in the right direction and bringing her back to the focal point when need be. Should you be interrupted by a third party, make a mental note of where you got to in her life story and then when you're alone again, remind her. She will be very impressed.

When she asks you about yourself keep it positive and up. If your life thus far has been steeped in horrific personal tragedy, keep it to yourself and focus only on the good bits. Lie if necessary. There's enough tragedy in the world without you adding more. Avoid past loves, being dumped, being fired or family deaths, and anything that smacks of negativity or bitterness in your life. And don't moan or whinge about your car, your job, the weather or whatever. Be completely positive and you will come over as a happy, well-adjusted, well-balanced soul.

13. **Sex talk.** Don't be afraid to talk about sex – everyone has an opinion on it and it's perennially fascinating, although we all generally try and 'do it' as opposed to talking about it. The topic of sex can be quite intoxicating and revealing, and elicit a variety of responses. Some women are open to it and can become very mischievous, trying to out-shock you. Others go red and clam up immediately. You'll know which one you're dealing with pretty quickly.

   The trick is knowing how to introduce the subject of sex into a conversation without turning her right off. You can't just say, 'Have you ever made love in the ocean?' or 'Do you masturbate?' or 'And what's *your* dildo called?' straight out of the blue, if at all.

   You need to first warm her up and then subtly challenge her into it. You can actually verbally bully her into talking about sex providing you keep within a respectful range of language and subject matter and are sensitive to her limits and body language. Talking about sex is exciting and dangerous and much more alive than talking about her cheesecake recipe. Her adrenalin will be pumping through her veins, her pubic temperature will rise and her hormones will certainly be awake and looking in your direction, checking you out.

   During a lull in your first wave of opening conversation throw in a curved ball like 'Tell me about your sex life.' It shows her that you're confident, unpredictable and really makes her sit up and take notice. You can actually watch her eyes widen and ears prick. Women usually respond surprisingly openly to brazen honesty. She might be slightly shocked but willing with a push. If she gags on her aperitif, back off a little and return to the subject later.

You might want to couch it slightly more softly by saying, 'Tell me about your love life' since the phrase 'love life' intones her current marital status and dating history as opposed to 'sex', which is more graphically explicit in the bedroom department.

Once you have her heading towards the subject you can pepper the conversation with casual but potent compliments that she will pick up on and unconsciously respond to. You will be able to tell immediately in her eyes whether or not you are embarrassing or insulting her. Initially she might be slightly coy or defensive and the conversation might go something like:

Her: 'Why should I tell you?'

You: 'I'm extremely interested. You're incredibly sexy and you strike me as being quite a sensual woman.' (If you mix the word 'sensual' with 'sexy', although 'sensual' is softer and more palatable, it takes on the same meaning.)

Her: 'Well, what particularly, do you want to know?'

At this point she has given you permission to delve. She has agreed to the rules and the game is definitely on. You'll find that once you get on to the subject of sex it's very difficult to get off it. If she asks something along the lines of 'What do you want to know?' or 'What can I tell you?' keep it open-ended and couch the conversation in broad strokes: 'Is there anything sexual that you've never tried?' or 'What kind of sex do you like?' or 'Have you ever been in control?'

14. **Service return.** She may turn the question back on you and say, 'Why don't you tell me about *your* sex life?' in which case tell her what she wants to hear. 'Well, I'm

pretty much in between women at the moment and was hoping that I might meet someone suitably gorgeous and sexy tonight. Someone just like you, in fact.' So now you've played your hand and the ball is well and truly back in her court.

15. **Modesty Blaze.** She may act reserved or modest and say something like, 'Oh dear, it's so uninteresting I wouldn't want to bore you with the details.' At which point you must raise your game and rise to the challenge. Basically if a woman you're attracted to tells you that her sex life is, or has recently been, boring, slow, non-existent, or anything else negative, then this is a thinly disguised plea for help in jazzing it up. The chances are if she readily admits that it is boring then it will probably be even worse than boring, i.e. a complete disaster. Clearly she's been mixing in the wrong circles and you, Sir Galahad, have finally arrived with the necessary finesse to change all that and show her a better tomorrow. Don't blow it.

You: 'I can't imagine a sexy woman like you having a boring sex life.'

16. **'What's your favourite fantasy?'** Once you get to this level then the sky has no limit. Here she is at liberty to invent any fantasy she wishes, which is both a measure of her inhibition as well as her imagination, coupled with her assessment of you and what she thinks you want to hear. She might want to shock you, she might play down her real fantasy and opt for the middle ground. If she says something ordinary like 'I'd like to make love under the stars' then her ceiling is pretty low and her vision narrow. Any woman over 21 who hasn't yet made love under the stars needs help. In this case

you could prise a wilder fantasy out of her by gently teasing her: 'That's pretty tame. I'm sure you've got a more daring fantasy than that.'

I once asked this of a complete stranger at a party more in a fit of mischief than any serious intent to score, and she gave me chapter and verse down to the very last detail of her ultimate sex fantasy which involved a large amount of eye-watering S&M and the odd billiards table. I almost choked on my Twiglets before saying, as casually as I could muster with a Twiglet lodged in my oesophagus, 'I think I could help you fulfil that fantasy, if you're interested.'

Mind games

17. **Yes, of course you're hitting on her.** You might get into a situation where the woman accuses you of trying to chat her up. 'Are you hitting on me?' she'll say, which would probably be delivered in a playful manner. There are a number of key responses but if she's being so up-front then don't disappoint her. Be upfront back. You might say, 'Well, I'm trying my best' or 'Well, I'd like to, yes, if you let me get a word in edgeways and stop interrupting me.' Always give as good as you get and she should do the same.

    Whatever you do don't get all defensive and fluster a pathetic, 'No, I'm not I'm …' Of course you are. And the sooner you let her know the better. You might want to probe: 'Does that agree with you or am I wasting my time?'

18. **Tell her you're temporarily impotent.** Another option is that when she accuses you of chatting her up, you might tell her not to worry and the reason you wouldn't even

attempt having sex with her is that you're slightly stressed at the moment and your penis is being very temperamental. Check her reaction but I'd be surprised if she wasn't curious to know more. Once you get the subject of sex onto a medical footing as opposed to an erotic one it's surprising how willing women are to talk about it and how opinionated they are.

Once you've spiked her interest, emphasise the fact that you would very much like to have sex with her and mention all the filthy things you would like to do to her (once your potency returns) to get her excited. If the conversation is going well, you might suggest that she try a controlled experiment whereby she tries to get you hard.

You must have seen that scene in *Trading Places* where Eddie Murphy pretends to be a cripple begging for money, kneeling on a trolley, and when the police come to move him along, he leaps up on to his legs and screams, 'Hallelujah, I can walk, I can walk. It's a miracle.' When your penis suddenly responds to her treatment, you can blame phantom past failures on not being with the right woman. She will feel like a heart surgeon who's just saved a patient's life.

19. **Impress her with your knowledge.** There's a way of letting her know you're clever or at least smart, without sounding like a know-it-all, which turns everyone right off immediately. Subtly weave your area of knowledge into the conversation but don't boast. Whatever you do don't use it to show off. Ease it in.

I was once at a party in America at the height of the Trivial Pursuits craze, and was stood with a collection of women and a real know-it-all who was banging on about Trivial Pursuits. He then asked the 'group' what he thought was the cleverest question of all: 'What is the capital city of Malta?' Americans are useless at geography but being a Brit, Valetta sprang immediately to mind and he shut up on the spot. Then I said, I've got one for you: 'What is the boiling point of mercury?' which I made up – the answer to which I haven't got a clue and don't know if mercury even boils. But it sounded terrific and he kept coming back at me all night with random temperatures: 'Five hundred degrees Centigrade?' Nope. 'Seven hundred and fifty degrees Celsius?' Nope. It was hilarious. When I whispered my little secret to the woman I was talking to, she collapsed in laughter and literally fell into my arms. She loved it.

Phone sense

Call early to avoid disappointment

We men generally leave that one important phone call until the last minute, which always works against us. It puts her under pressure since she's probably already made arrangements. Yes, spontaneity is brilliant, and to be admired, but, these days, with a busy woman in a busy city you need to book early to be assured of success. You need to speak to a woman in good time if you are going to ask her out for the coming weekend because she needs time to organise her diary and her wardrobe. If you leave it until Friday to ask her out on a date for Saturday then don't be surprised if she says she can't make it.

It's better to plan at least four days in advance, better still a week, to avoid the disappointment of that initial 'no'. Even if she says, 'I'd love to, but …' you're already on the back foot and trying to recover; which will dent your confidence and put you off trying again.

Rather get in early and keep it loose, saying something like 'I'd love to meet you for a drink – are you around in the next week?'

Not calling her

I'm amazed at how many men get quite far down the line with a woman and then back out or get an attack of pure laziness. You've gone to the trouble of getting to talk to her and get her phone number, which she gave enthusiastically, and now you won't do anything about it. Duh! Women never understand this, and it drives them insane. This is like having a ticket to the Cup Final and not using it.

Reasons why you're not calling

- **You changed your mind.** Did you really change your mind about her or are you just using this as an excuse?

- **Cold feet.** What if she's changed her mind? What if she was just giving you her number to appease you? What if it's the wrong number? Look, forget all these what-ifs and stop torturing yourself. You are never going to know one way or the other until you call her. So do it.

- **You don't know what to say.** Come now. She gave you her telephone number which is a personal invitation for a private party between the two of you. You must have spoken to her already and made a positive impression to get the number, so don't cave in now. Women love chatting on the phone about complete rubbish for hours, so all you have to do is dial, say, 'Hi, I've been thinking about you. What have you been up to?' and she'll do the rest. You probably won't get a word in edgeways for the next thirty minutes.

> **TIP:** *Call from a landline.*

- **You don't really fancy her.** Is this true or is this simply another excuse? Remember earlier we agreed that you can never know enough women? Consequently it might be a good idea if you at least call her and keep her warm and sweet. You can always tell her that you're going to be away for a week on business, until you decide what you want to do with her. This gives you an opportunity to be very sweet on the phone, as in 'Sorry about this, I was really looking forward to seeing you. I thought you looked fantastic the other night' or words to that effect.

  And the week away buys you time to think clearly.

> **TIP:** *If you do call and tell her you're going away, call her again mid-week and tell her you were thinking of her and have just called to see if she's still interested in getting together sometime.*

> **NOTE:** *Don't call before first getting some details on the place you're supposed to be at. Don't try and describe the foyer of the George Cinq Hotel in Paris if you've never been there.*

- **You can't decide on a decent idea for a date.** You don't need to. Keep it casual. Just say, 'Do you fancy getting together at the weekend some time?' She will invariably have something on during the weekend but, unless she's Martha Stewart, she will undoubtedly have some time free, and, assuming that she wants to see you, she will probably push out shopping with her mate Doreen in favour of you.

- **You're waiting for a better offer.** You can wait and wait and wait for ever. Just like it's easier to get another job when you're in a job, it's much easier to meet another girlfriend when you've got one. So if you've got the opportunity to get a girlfriend, grab it. Apart from the obvious physical benefits – while you're waiting – it's great practice. And just being seen with a girl ups your attraction rating. The inference being, he must have something. The trick is to get in the game, shake your double six and get on the board, and then get an upgrade if and when the opportunity arises. If you're not on the board you're nowhere.

Send her an SMS

Sting and the police should redo the single sending out an SOS and replace it with SMS; the SMS (text) is the fastest, most immediate and intimate form of communication and you can even send her a photo down the phone along with it to remind her of your rampant good looks. Not only is texting fabulously fast and loaded with the cleverness of new technology, it allows you to flirt outrageously and get an immediate response. It also allows you to hide behind technology in that she won't hear your breathless whisper or pick up on your nervous um-ing and ah-ing – or excitement when she says yes. It's something you can do any time of the day or night since she doesn't have to answer until she wants to. In fact it's a good trick to text her in the middle of the night since yours will be the first text message she gets when she checks her mobile phone in the morning. You can be very daring in a text message which no other messaging and communication system allows.

- Are you awake?
- Been thinking of you.
- Do you want to come over?

• Can't wait to see you …

• Got chocolate in the fridge.

• I love you.

However, if like David Beckham you're married or otherwise attached, bear in mind that text messages can be a lethal time bomb in the hands of the recipient if you should ever fall out with her – as David discovered with Rebecca Loos.

TIP 1: *If you're going out with somebody younger than 20, then you might text them in their preferred lingo like 'Gr8 2 c u' (great to see you) but with anyone over 25 I'd suggest writing out the words fully, or almost fully. It shows that you're taking the time and conveys more feeling since it sounds more sincere. Over time you can develop your mutual private and personal language and code. For instance, one friend uses the code NORWICH (knickers off ready when I come home), and other lewder offerings when texting his girlfriend.*

TIP 2: *Flirt outrageously with a girl via text messaging, but when you ask her out, do it face to face, or at least live on the phone.*

WORKSHOP 4
The holiday affair is a specialist skill

First know this

Women are notoriously gregarious and generous when they are on holiday, and are as much looking for you as you are for them.

One friend in the travel industry put it thus: 'The women take their knickers off at Malaga airport and only put them back on two weeks later.' That 18–30 mentality kicks in and the tabloids have had a feast every year reporting on the shagging that goes on along the Costa del Sol and everywhere else for that matter. Your opportunity to score on holiday is probably 100 per cent better than it is at home on a normal Friday night. Women are relaxed, in a good mood, away from home and willing to give you the benefit of the doubt. Providing you look halfway decent and haven't got your eyes stuck to her breasts. When braless women wander about in wispy nothingness, breasts jumping about like two kittens in a fight, it's virtually impossible not to stare. The least you can do is put your tongue back in your mouth and calm down. There is a skill in approaching, chatting up and seducing a woman on holiday. And drooling is not part of the repertoire. Salivating, ogling and smartass sexist comments will only serve to destroy any promising first impression.

So grab your towel, your suntan lotion and your flip-flops and read on before you blow it.

Don't waste any time whatsoever

Because you haven't got much time to lose. Babes are arriving and disappearing every day. So you can't afford to hesitate – your right woman could be here today and gone tonight and you'll kick yourself if you miss her. If you see the potential mother of your children waltzing down the beach you need to get in there fast.

Make contact and not just eye contact

Check her out and if you get a positive response – raised eyebrows, smile, playing with her hair, blows you a kiss (optimist) – even a half response, don't wait for a written invitation or stub your toes in the sand, get over there. 'Hi, how long have you been here?' or 'What hotel are you staying at?' and 'When are you leaving?' are the usual openers. Once you're chatting you might want to stop mid-sentence and say, 'You have a fabulous smile' before continuing. The next thing is to ascertain where she is from.

> **TIP:** *Try and pick somebody within batting distance of where you live.*

Avoid childish behaviour

Lobbing a football or rugby ball onto the back of her topless torso and then saying sorry while retrieving the ball and trying not to stare at her breasts is what 12-year-olds do, and does not make for a positive vibe. Rather tell her you're a man short for your volleyball team and you think she looks suitably athletic. By the time you've taught her how to serve overarm, she might teach you a thing or two.

Ask her friends about her

Speed things up by making her friend do all the work for you. Be extremely blunt. Wait until the girl you fancy moves to the loo or the bar and go over and say, 'Hi, I fancy your mate. What are my chances?' This can go either way. Maybe she's called Daphne and hasn't had a boyfriend in eight years. Alternatively her boyfriend, who has just done two years in Parkhurst for GBH, might be arriving soon. It's always a risk but it's well worth taking.

Lose your mates

If you have a bevy of loyal, loveable but socially retarded mates, try and lose them during that slightly embarrassing, heavy duty, wooing stage when you're trying to seduce that gorgeous blonde into thinking that you are indeed a solvent, upstanding citizen with high moral fibre and a BMW Z4 (back home).

Use your mates

Decide on which of you has what skill with women and devise a strategy accordingly. Who has the looks, the chat, the charm, the money, the car, etc. and how will you divide up the spoils? When faced with a group of women always send the least dashing of your mates in to bat first. Preferably Eric who has spots and isn't that interested in sex anyway. He can do a reconnaissance and make a fool of himself before you move in to apologise for his awkward over-familiarity. As the evening progresses it's every man for himself.

7
Personal ads and Internet dating

Twelve years ago I was so bored with my mate moaning about his lack of luck with women, that I wrote a personal ad for him and put it in the 'Lonely Hearts' section of *Loot* (at my own expense). The response was modest – five replies, one of which included a used condom with the words 'This is what the last guy left me' written on a card; but out of the other four sane replies, he had success with two. In any direct-marketing endeavour 50 per cent is considered an extremely high success rate and this prompted him to embark on a decade-long personal ad campaign that would have impressed Maurice Saatchi.

Luckily for him, as he became better at it and he refined his personal ad technique, the dating game changed and it became respectable and commonplace to use the personal ads to augment other more traditional dating mechanisms. Ten years ago, if you put an ad in a personal column you were thought of as a loser and a complete social cretin (which he was, of course). And you would certainly have kept quiet about it, hoping you never got asked that dinner-party staple: 'And where did you two meet?'

The early, classic *Time Out* personal columns were always more homo than hetero and very hippy-trippy brown rice, but there were few other outlets apart from *Loot* where you could advertise for a half-decent girl and hope to get a half-decent response.

Today, personal columns are an accepted, clever and timely way of meeting the opposite sex and there is no shortage of outlets, from *The Times* to your local paper. The genre has exploded in its sophistication and outlets.

It makes sense to use every available opportunity to connect with the opposite sex. Our lifestyles have speeded up to the point where there's hardly time to grab a sandwich and have a pee, and there is far less time to meet women through the conventional channels, i.e. being introduced (does anybody do that any more?) or literally bumping into somebody at a pub or club.

Then came the Internet and the personal column has moved up yet another gear. This is state-of-the-art speed dating. You can connect 24 hours a day 7 days a week.

Benefits of a personal ad in the newspaper or on the Internet

- **It's working when and where you're not.** While you're sleeping, some single, lonely or curious woman out there, in a place you will never normally go to, could be checking out your ad, building a mild fantasy around you and responding to your ad. That's quite an unbelievable bonus.

- **Wide audience.** The audience is infinite and the beauty of it is that you are reaching a fresh audience almost daily as the membership churns. It is huge.

- **Precisely targeted.** You can more accurately focus your efforts on a certain kind of woman or geographical location. There are so many sites and variations on the theme, if you wanted to attract a 32-year-old Scandinavian mathematician with a pet parrot and a liking for Italian food, the chances are there's a site where you can reach her. This is very useful if you're moving overseas or to a new area. You can post an ad on the local website along the lines of 'Brit relocating to South Africa, seeks new women friends in the Cape Town area'. This gives you the added kudos of being 'new' and gives you a temporary edge. Half the women in Cape Town will regard you as fresh meat and will want to get in early.

- **Sell yourself.** It allows you to sell yourself better than you ever can face to face. This is particularly helpful if you are shy or lacking in social grace. This means that you can establish a real bond, open up and feel comfortable with someone before you get to spend time in front of them.

- **Intimacy.** You can be far more intimate and honest, and say infinitely more in a letter or e-mail, than you ever will initially over the phone or when you meet face to face.

- **Screening process.** Many of the sites do the preliminary screening for you, electronically checking thousands of ads for your perfect match … well, what they consider to be your perfect match, although even the best sites still cough up a motley crew of assorted boilers. However, there are some surprising gems to be found. Even Internet dating is hard work and you will need to sift through hundreds of ads before finding your true love. But these are women who you would not normally meet. Just think of how many bars and night classes and friends you would need to frequent to get exposure to this many women.

The downside

The Internet is full of nutters and you could find that that gorgeous blonde with big tits who claims to be a cordon bleu cook from Ross-on-Wye, turns out to be Mad Steve dialling in from the Broadmoor library computer. This is a scenario which, if you've been e-mailing her/him for the past month and getting excited about meeting her/him, is incredibly frustrating.

Again though, you can waste a lot of time and money advertising in the wrong place and in the wrong way if you're not careful. Pick your media carefully. First research the genre thoroughly. You will find that it is easy to get burned. There are a few rules of engagement if you are to be successful at it, without paying a fortune in money or time.

There are some serious syndicates who work the personals for profit and gain or ID theft, so watch out. Especially watch out for Eastern Bloc babes who post an absolutely gorgeous photo of themselves (mm, is that really you?) and ask for you to send her the odd fiver to help with her 'expenses'. These girls all seem to have degrees in medicine from St Petersburg University, although they generally misspell medicine and, unfortunately – surprise, surprise – find themselves 'waitressing at this moment in time'. Oh, and did she tell you about the three-year-old daughter?

> **TIP:** *Never part with any cash before you meet.*

Tips on how to write a decent online and personal ad

- **Make *every* word count.** You only have a set number of words or characters (letters and spaces) so get your ad as tight as possible. Leave out long or pretentious words and redundant connecting words that don't say or add anything. Stop beating about the bush. Rather than: 'Man in the prime of his life would genuinely like to meet an attractive woman who loves the outdoors', say 'Thirty-something man seeks outdoorsy woman', and then use the other words or characters to say something that's actually interesting and different. To save words, run things on rather than start a new sentence, e.g. '… outdoorsy woman who adores cooking, jazz, hang-gliding and old movies'.

- **Be different and original.** Check out the small ads and you'll find that 80 per cent use the same boring tack and are practically interchangeable. 'Attractive' is the most over-used adjective in the history of personal ads. It's meaningless. Who says they are attractive, their mother? Attractive to who? And anyway, everyone thinks of themselves as attractive in some way. Try and write something that engages and entertains, that leaves the reader with a wry smile and wanting more.

- **Be honest.** The more honest you are the less time, and money, you waste. It might seem fun to lead some truly gorgeous babe on by making her think that you are Mr Dashing Polo Player, when you are really Mr Overweight

Panel-beater, or by sending her, or posting, a 'genuine' photo of yourself that was actually taken in the 1980s when you still had hair and decent eyesight. This defeats the object and is unfair on her and yourself. You will be the one who, eventually, will be found out and miserably rejected. Why waste time when you stand a chance of meeting someone who is genuinely interested in you for you? Who loves your bald patch and bottle-bottomed spectacles?

- **Be specific.** Many ads are extremely loose and goosy, and say nothing. If you want a woman who's interested in having children, or who likes chess, or having her bottom spanked, say so. Describe what kind of relationship you're looking for: long term, marriage, recreational sex, fun.

- **Don't show off.** Everybody hates a show-off. Even if you do own half of Herefordshire and have a holiday home in the Maldives, keep that under your hat until your next stage of communication. 'Oh, by the way, I forgot to tell you I have a small place in the Maldives' dropped into conversation on your second date will carry so much more weight. 'Shall we go sometime?'

- **Post a photo.** It's a natural reaction to check out the photo ads first, so immediately you're giving yourself a huge advantage by posting one and putting yourself at a severe disadvantage by not posting one. Make sure it's recent, that you look your best and have no off-putting or controversial props inadvertently in the picture, i.e. like a topless poster of Jordan.

Responding to an ad

Dos and don'ts when writing a response

Try and mirror the wording of the ad she has written and deal with each of her points before launching into a 15-page monologue about yourself. In fact, forget the 15-page monologue. This is the equivalent of 'listening' and shows you have taken time to consider her wishes and requirements, and taken note of her dreams and hobbies.

Also, try and avoid sending out the same response to every girl in town. It shows and doesn't sound genuine. It will have a hollow ring to it. Once you've established mutual interest, try and transfer this to get visual or verbal contact as soon as possible.

The webcam – seeing is believing

To make this even more interesting and intriguing and much more honest and real, get a webcam. If she hasn't got one urge her to get one or, if you're feeling flash, buy her one at Dixon's online and have it delivered to her address. Then there's no excuse. You can learn a lot about a person by the room she's in and what's in it. Ask her to detach it from its plinth and wave it about the room. Concentrate now. Oh no, she's got fifty cuddly toys on her bed. And what's that photo of Buddha? She might want to entice you by revealing various interesting parts of her anatomy ('I don't believe you've got a tattoo on your bum. Show me then …') but I'll leave that to your power of persuasion.

> **TIP:** *There's this website www.eyeballchat.com where you can download a thing called eyeball chat which allows you to chat in real time – well, a virtual, ticker-tape conversation, as you are watching. Neat.*

The statistics make interesting reading

I read on one dating website that 25 per cent of the ads get 90 per cent of the hits. This is because they are either worded intriguingly or they contain a photo. People always read ads with a photo first. A photo saves a lot of time and the 'disappointment factor' when someone connects with the image of 'tall dark and handsome' and ends up with 'short fat and balding'.

The meeting

With either offline or online personal ads, when it comes to the big meeting, as with any date, there is always a sense of apprehension. You now know a lot about each other to the point where you are willing to risk a meeting. You've probably been e-mailing or snail-mailing each other for weeks now, and have built up a thorough profile of each other and a mutual fantasy of what should happen. It's quite a nerve-wracking moment since although you know each other well you're doing everything back to front: you've put in the spade work and now you want to know that her promised looks and body fit your required image of her. Has she been honest? Like really honest? There's an awful dread of that phrase 'Before we go any further, there's something I forgot to tell you.'

Recruiting a little help – the softer options

Speed dating

Another imported New York phenomenon, speed dating, involves joining a group of anything from 10–20 single hopefuls at a pre-arranged venue for a series of five- to ten-minute interviews with each person. The hope is that within those few minutes you will connect with at least one of the other singles, and on the back of that fix up a proper date. It's a relatively new thing but a crop of new agencies have sprung up and it's presently quite trendy.

However, the range of ages is often quite wide and needs to be tailored to specific age ranges. Also, the social and professional mix can be a trifle forced and again needs to at least reflect groups that might be interested in each other.

> **TIP:** *Before you sign up ask for an indication of who else is on the guest list, or at least what type of people they are.*

Five minutes is not a long time – about the length of an average news bulletin on the radio – and it's difficult even for eloquent souls to spit out what it is they do and do not want, and what they are looking for, in such a short space of time. It's interesting here that the women tend to talk about what they want and the men sit there trying to sell them what they have to offer.

The trick here is to be brutally honest and if you do fancy someone just sit there and say something like, 'I don't know about you but I'm sold. I think you are completely right for me. You're the kind of woman I've been looking for, for ages. How about we go for a drink after this and get to know each other better?'

> **NOTE:** *If you say that to each of your ten interviewees you'd probably get a yes out of at least two.*

Dinner clubs
Allied to speed dating, although a little slower, is the singles dining club where a group of 20 or so singles meet at a

restaurant on an informal, though managed 'date'. The theory here is that you get a decent crack at meeting somebody at least relevant and you have more time to nourish and nurture that connection.

The benefit is that you get to eat a decent meal and drink a half-decent bottle of wine while the conversation is full flowing and not stilted. The only problem is the musical-chairs element, where you are forced to rotate seating arrangements after each course, or halfway through. This is acutely annoying if you've already met your *right woman* and you now have to leave her sitting next to some handsome hunk.

The dating agency – the human touch

The dating agency is considered a more traditional, rather quaint and old-fashioned service in these hi-tech days of instant Internet dating; but it does have its strengths and can be another useful addition to your dating arsenal. The personal touch can offer a much more subtle approach, while that third-party involvement can add 'intelligence' and insider knowledge to the proceedings, saving you a lot of time and money.

Did you see that story last March about the Swiss multi-millionairess who was looking for a boyfriend/husband through a dating agency in Zurich? The report didn't mention what she looked like or whether she was fat or thin – it simply said that she was some industrial heiress, worth a couple of billion, who was lonely and had decided to get proactive about finding a new man. The next day the agency was inundated with suitors from all over the world. Moral of this mini-story is: if you want to meet a rich woman, join a Zurich dating agency.

Each dating agency has its own style and personality ranging from casual but professional to very self important, and this corresponds with the type of people the agency attracts: older women, professional women, Jewish, Christian, millionairesses, single mothers, young 18–30s, those who just want sex (one agency just puts married people seeking an affair in touch with each other). There's something for everyone because, in the dating game, niching is king.

Of these hundreds of agencies trying to play Cupid, most of them are pretty established and will throw up a succession of reasonably suitable babes for a price. Some are just glorified knocking shops and some are pretty sad, with catalogues full of tragic or forgotten plain Janes who were sidelined from the fast track years ago and have never recovered. Mostly, though, if you join the right agency it can be a very rich, effortless source of female talent. It's just another solution to add to your repertoire. Check where they advertise and you'll get a better idea of what type of women they are attracting.

Talk to the mother

Every agency has its matriarch. Don't think of this Mother Hen as a nosy bitch and an intruder into your private life. She's only doing her job and if she's good at it, she will find you a good date faster than you will yourself. If you relax and tell her exactly what you're looking for, then she should deliver. She'll say, 'I think you'd be a perfect match for Pandora' and off you go.

Go to a reputable agency

The trick here is to find out which one works for you and you can only do this by nipping along for the customary interview and having a chat with the Mother Hen. Generally, the more expensive the agency, the better quality the date, but this is not always the case. Some agencies that charge a small fortune can still throw up a stable of seriously desperate boilers.

Check out the goods

Take a quick scan of who they have on their books and what type of women they specialise in. Don't be swayed by that one shot of a gorgeous healthy blonde in their ad. It is probably a stock picture.

Don't part with any cash

Until you've checked out the number and calibre of the women they have on the books. Also you need to know precisely how many dates you get for your membership and what the hidden costs are. What is in the small print? Generally the cost is quite steep, but you get what you pay for, or should at least.

Stick to the rules

Some of the women are real tell-tales (which is probably why they are still on the books) and if you're late, don't say the right thing or don't stick to the protocol or the dress code, they complain bitterly to the Mother Hen. Although, if you've half a brain, you pretty quickly get the politics waxed.

Be warned

With some of the lesser agencies, there is a tendency to try and market the back catalogue first – if a woman has been on the books for a while, hasn't had any offers and is moaning about her membership fee, they may throw her a bone by using you (i.e. dashing, new, fresh meat) to appease her. Woof! Down boy!

The darker side

Chip away at the underbelly of society and you will find a dark place where things are very different from the run-of-the-mill dating scene, and the average personal ad website. It's up to you where you draw your personal moral and sexual stance but it's good to know that there is 'another option' and there are plenty of women who inhabit a world that is regarded as extremely 'kinky', not normally accessed by so-called 'respectable' folk. Some of these women are very attractive and extremely, overtly sexual. The 'S&M movement' and its acceptability is growing, so even greater numbers of attractive women are experimenting with their personal brand of sexuality within the scene.

London-based Skin 2 was one of the forerunners of the S&M scene. It's been going for years now and is an international institution. The magazine, the fetish clothing, the 'club' and their annual 'rubber ball' have all become more acceptable to a broader audience than their original handful of dominatrix and underground contributors. Now that designers like Jean Paul Gaultier have incorporated S&M and fetish themes into their clothing, and many shops like Agent Provocateur and Anne Summers have gained solid 'respectability', Skin 2 itself has become pretty mainstream.

High sexual energy

This means that 'normal' average guys can go along to clubs like Torture Garden, Submission, The Slimelight or Rendezvous and immerse themselves in what is a truly extraordinary and fascinating spectacle without being considered a pervert. If you've never been to this type of club it is quite an experience and the air is charged with a high sexual energy, with everyone wondering around half-naked wearing a nonsense of PVC, leather and satin in a celebration of exhibitionism, voyeurism, fetish worship and sexual liberation. There really is something for everyone.

> **NOTE:** *The names and locations of these clubs change by the minute so call Skin 2 for an update.*

Know the protocol

It may sound like a free-for-all but there is a certain protocol attached to meeting people and although the woman at the bar may have her bare breasts sticking out of a leather basque, it is not the done thing to sidle up and start tweaking her nipples. This is not a normal nightclub so forget everything you would say and do there. Those rules no longer apply.

In fact, the people are generally very polite and surprisingly controlled and well behaved. You really need to go a few times and observe what goes on before you get actively involved, or you could make a naïve faux pas. What you don't want is to send out the wrong signals and suddenly find yourself locked in a remote antechamber chained to a wall with a peroxide blonde whacking your ass with a studded leather paddle.

What is surprising is how 'normal' Jane, who has a chain around her neck and practically little else, is on the 'outside'. I once met a fabulous environmental lawyer dressed in a maid's outfit and enjoyed several interesting months trawling these clubs with her until she eventually moved to Brussels to save the planet. Having a woman actively enjoy wearing the fantasy uniform of stockings and suspenders, lacy basques and ridiculously high heels, when you normally have to beg other women to get into anything more exotic than a pair of French knickers ('Do I really have to, they're so uncomfortable?'), is like starring in your own blue movie. And the whole S&M fetish scene is loaded with a surreal, taboo form of sexual excitement I've personally never experienced anywhere else.

Once you get plugged in to this world and fine-tuned into the network, then you will find all sorts of opportunities to meet a very different type of woman and see a very different side to the 'normal' woman you thought she was.

Be warned though

There are different levels of involvement, from pure self-indulgent peacocking in high-fetish fashion, to plumbing a seriously perverse depth which some readers may find offensive and not want to ever reach, even in the darkest basement of their dreams. In New York, for instance, there are a few select clubs with names like The Vault and Hell's Kitchen in the meat-packing area on Lower 9th Street that will make your eyes water.

Not for the faint-hearted, they tend to move around every six months or so in terms of location, so you need to plug into the magazines and websites to stay up to date. Once you've been you should have a contact number where you can call for the next 'party' whenever you're in town.

Allied to the clubs are the websites and their attendant personal ads. These again are quite different from the run-of-the-mill lonely hearts, in that you certainly won't be innocently swapping favourite hobby stories about stamp collecting and horse-riding. These are heavy duty and explicitly sexual, but wickedly intoxicating.

Dog and bone

Dogging is another great British institution – just taking the dog for a walk past the odd lover's lane where there just happens to be a variety of couples indulging in public sex and an orgy of group sex and voyeurism. The nation has seemingly gone dogging mad of late and there is a situation, if you are given to such tastes (and this is something I have never tried myself), whereby you can cruise one of the many dogging websites in the morning and be having wild sex in the evening with a perfect stranger at the bottom of your local cemetery.

WORKSHOP 5
Taming the female 'Romeo' (when a shag is just a shag)

Sex has been elevated or relegated – whichever way you look at it – to a non-spectator recreational sport along with squash and tennis. Sex is the acceptable new way to keep mind and body active, alert and functioning properly. Sex is trendy. Consequently women are more open to casual sex than they ever were as long as the rules are set out and agreed upon, and, more often than not, as long as they are the ones setting the rules.

The adult social sit-com *Sex in the City*, in which four girl 'friends' fuck their way around New York, and over-analyse the consequences, has gone a long way to free women up in terms of satisfying their own sexual needs. All accomplished career women – the lawyer, the writer, the PR executive and the gallery owner – they all celebrated the freedom that post-feminist society gave to women, but at the end of the day they were all desperately seeking that elusive Holy Grail that everybody else is seeking: love.

In the meantime, though, the knowledge that even the most promiscuous woman is searching for her *right man*, *right now* is little comfort when confronted with that woman going through her sex-in-the-city stage. For once the boot is firmly on the other foot, i.e. you fall in love with her and she treats you like a one-night stand.

'Oh, it was only a shag,' she says as you, thinking her the ultimate uber-babe, blubber pathetic pleas into your mobile phone and prepare to slit your wrists. It's something men have been doing to women for years but it's only recently that modern women have actively and openly included it in their social repertoire. This can happen at any age and any circumstance.

Watch for those women with a fly-in, fly-out lifestyle: sales reps, businesswomen, air hostesses and any woman who isn't in one place long enough to face the consequences of her actions. It's interesting that over 40 per cent of business travellers these days are now women. Also, women who have recently been divorced usually get a new lease of life and will enjoy playing the field for a short spell after their split.

The justification is that now, in progressive circles, sex is regarded more of a bodily 'release', i.e. a health benefit, which can be built into a weekly routine along with the pedicure and reflexology, rather than the traditional, old-fashioned view of sex being a woman 'prostituting' herself to please the man.

Being coldly chewed up and spat out by some fiery sex bomb can come as quite a shock and be a profound disappointment if you were hoping for something more substantial from that one woman, but recognise it for what it is. You can have great sex with someone who is hot and fancies you but who is not necessarily romantically interested in you. Great sex is good for the soul so bite the bullet and just go with the flow. And great sex is far superior to watching another video rerun of Manchester United versus Arsenal on your own with leftover pizza.

How to change her mind

When a woman is in this promiscuous phase of her life, i.e. her *Sex in the City* phase, and is seemingly cutting a swathe through half the male race in cavalier fashion, it is futile to offer her a garland of daisies and hope to change her mind. She's consumed with the power she has over men and is currently enjoying flaunting that power. The good news is that it is normally only a 'phase', which means it is temporary and she will eventually change her own mind or grow out of it. Best strategy here, if you really want to get under her skin and stay there and have something concrete to show for your effort is:

- **Have great sex.** She wants great sex, so give her what she wants. No mamby-pambying around either, don't over-analyse it or waste time feeling guilty, just get down and dirty. Show her how sexually adventurous you are or are willing to be. Make no demands on her other than that she orgasms frequently and maybe wears a nice set of lacy stockings and suspenders. Oh and don't forget to wear a condom.

- **Vocalise your interest.** Let her know that you are very keen on her (but whatever you do, don't go all soppy and tell her you love her at this stage). Discuss your situation in broad strokes, half-jokingly, in your post-coital slumber. Be honest about it without pressurising her by saying something loose but loaded like, 'If you ever grow out of your shopping-and-fucking phase I'd really like to make an honest woman of you.' Try not to be intimidated by the other men she is seeing and never ask what they're like in comparison to yourself. This could be difficult if your sex keeps getting interrupted by calls from Eric on her mobile phone but let it ride. Turn her phone off for her. For the moment, think of her as a welcome treat that drops into your life now and again.

- **Keep tabs on her.** Monitor her at regular intervals and gauge her mood and 'phase'. Don't let her disappear off the radar. Meet her as often as you can get away with without turning into her personal lapdog. Try and build a friendship, or at least a firmer bond, by allowing her to see other sides of your personality, other than your propensity to stay hard and shag well.

- **Watch for the 'snap'.** It may take a while but eventually she will tire of bonking half of Bedfordshire and see herself as shallow and empty.

> **NOTE:** *This will be a sudden sea change after some road-to-Damascus enlightenment either from a friend, a self-help*

book, a TV show or a possible health scare. (Nothing terri-
fies a woman or switches a woman off casual sex faster than
a dose of something painful or embarrassing in the vagina
dept.) Whatever it is, something will trigger her change of
heart, at which point she will no longer be just looking for a
shag, but something more substantial. You may find her
suddenly calling you out of the blue with a much less aggres-
sive stance.

- **Be there for her when she switches.** At this point avoid
  getting all cocky and saying things like 'I knew you'd come
  around eventually', or 'Couldn't resist me. Huh? I knew I'd get
  you in the end.' Remain cool and marginally aloof, and work on
  moving your relationship to a more traditionally romantic footing by incorporating the fun and more innocent pre-sex elements of dating that you've been missing, like going to a
  movie, out for dinner, or a walk along the beach.

- **Know this.** If you persist and reach this stage then you will
  have the comfort of knowing that if she does decide on you as
  a partner, then it is a very genuine choice. Having successfully
  passed through her Sex in the City phase and got the other
  men out of her system, you could look forward to a long-
  lasting, loyal relationship.

TIP: If some other guy is pursuing the same strategy you could
employ the fear close. Let her know that you've found somebody else you're interested in who is equally gorgeous, and subtly urge her to make her mind up – the inference being that
although you're keen and have waited patiently for her, time is
running out. This usually has the effect of forcing

her to do an emotional stocktake during which, if all goes according to plan, she will realise what a 'catch' she has in you and how much she doesn't want to lose you. The risk, of course, is that she chooses Eric.

8
The date

'It's such a refreshing change to meet a man who can take 'yes' for an answer'

You need to plan the date, not her

Pre-plan

The best policy is to have a game plan in mind before you even ask her out. What are you going to do with her if she says 'yes'? Once you've got her to say 'yes' to a date with you, you can ruin the whole moment by asking, 'What would you like to do?' Don't ask a woman where she wants to go on a date. You, the man, must decide. Surprise her. Intrigue her. Let her know that you've got something 'special' up your sleeve. The trick is for the woman not to have to think about where you're going, at what time and how you're going to get there. That's your job. Her job is to say 'yes' and turn up, on time, or a fashionable ten minutes late, looking sexy and gorgeous and smelling delicious.

The three-dates-to-heaven process explained

First date

Meet her somewhere safe and public during the day, so there's no excuse for you to even try to get her into bed. It's innocent and unpressured. Make it a quick lunch or 'event' – maybe a walk around an art gallery or a sandwich in the park if it's a hot day. This is the innocent, get-to-know-you-better date. Give her a social kiss when you part and make a follow-up date for two nights' time to go to the movies, dinner or whatever.

Second date

Make this a mid-week evening date so you have an excuse to leave early, leaving her wanting more. You have the date, you get on really well and when you drop her off or you part, you should have reached a First Kiss meltdown. Calm down. Say something very encouraging like, 'I really enjoyed that. I love being with you' and make a follow-up date for the Friday or Saturday night. Look, if she invites you in for a *coffee* you can either a) make an excuse like, 'I'd love to but I need to finish a proposal for tomorrow morning', and leave her wanting more (if she's keen now she'll be even keener on Saturday), or b) what the hell, dive in and see how it goes. If she's keen now, she's keen now. Don't look a gift horse in the mouth. It's your call.

Bingo night

Assuming she didn't invite you in for coffee, then this third, 'weekend date' is the big one. You should have chatted in the meantime and mentally prepared her for a big night. Neither of you are under any false illusions – if all goes well on the date, this is the stopover and breakfast will be served. So stock up the fridge with tasty nibbly bits and champagne if you can afford it.

Taking advantage of the concept of 'implied consent'

Once you have a date for a weekend night, you need to get her to agree to do something with you the following morning, such as a wander around Portobello Road, or go for a coffee at Harvey Nichols. This is implied consent – basically, you've organised the beginning and the end so the embarrassing middle bit, i.e. SEX, is taken for granted.

Greetings

When you meet a woman on a date for the first time, whether you meet at the bus stop or the foyer of the Ritz, whatever you do, don't reach out your hand for a handshake. You're not doing business in Osaka. Next thing you know, you'll be swapping business cards. Reach out and touch her upper arms and pull her gently towards you (I said 'gently' – it's not arm-wrestling) and give her a quick peck on the cheek. There, you've kissed her. Don't wait for her to do something or you'll still be standing there an awkward two metres apart in 2010. Say something like, 'It's great to see you.' And then compliment her on something. This woman has probably spent five hours getting ready, so the least you can do is notice. 'You look fantastic. I love what you've done with your hair', or whatever. A woman always tends to favour an item that is special to her, which could be earrings or pearls, a favourite jacket or shoes. Pick up on it. 'Those shoes are amazing.'

Phrases to avoid saying

'Would you mind if I asked you a question?' You have just asked her a question. So just ask the question. Starting off by asking her permission to ask her out is not the way to go. Next it's 'Would you mind awfully if I kissed you?' This is negative and uncertain talk and sends out the message that you are unsure and unconfident, which is not an attractive quality for a woman to find in a man. Women like their men to come complete with a backbone. Also it puts the onus, the decision-making, back in her court, which women don't like. She doesn't think she should be the one to decide whether or not you should kiss her. Stop being so fair and democratic – this isn't the United Nations, it's a romance. Just kiss her.

Be dangerous

Don't get me wrong – I don't mean you have to drive your car off a cliff for kicks. But the act of experiencing something that is either scary or dangerous has been found to cement a bond between you. It's good that you're afraid. That means you're going somewhere where you've never been before. That's how half the relationships got going in the 1950s – the f-word then was 'f' for fairgrounds, big wheels and rides that scared the shit out of the women and allowed the men to put their strong arms around them and be brave.

Read her body language

Whether a woman is in a bar, on a train or shopping, if she is attracted to you her body can't help revealing that attraction. There are seven key ways in which you can subtly tell a woman is interested in you:

1. **Positioning.** She opens up her body to you by turning towards you, allowing you to get a good view of her.

2. **Flicks her hair.** She will tease or flick her hair away from

her face to expose her face and neck.

3. **Licks her lips.** And I don't mean movie star deliberate – this is unconscious and she doesn't know she's doing it. She is wetting her lips ready for engagement.

4. **Looks at you and looks down or away.** She wants to convey interest but not overdo it.

5. **Points her foot at you.** If she dangles her shoe off her toes, then you're in.

6. **Smiles.** Once she smiles then you need to determine which kind of smile it was – merely pleasant and friendly or sexually charged. If she raises her eyebrows in a come-on gesture she's screaming, 'What are you waiting for?' Well, what are you waiting for – a written invitation from the Pope? Get over there fast.

7. **Touching.** Once in her personal zone, if she touches you on the arm or wrist you may as well book the hotel now.

Mind your body language

I was watching a young guy try and chat up a girl on the beach the other day and although he had the looks and the body and the undivided interest of the woman, who was hot-looking and hot for him, he blew it. He was shuffling his feet in the sand like a naughty four-year-old schoolboy, fidgeting with his hands and looking down and away, but never at the woman. He had positioned himself about two yards away from her. Every time she moved nearer to him, he made a step backwards away from her. In the end, she got bored and gave up on him.

Eye contact

Eye contact is probably the most important facet of body language, since each of you can transmit so much and pick up so much from the subtle changes in eye language. As they are considered to be the windows of the soul, it's difficult to lie through heavily scrutinised eyes. Look at her when she's talking and when you're talking to her. Just look at her all the time. Resist the urge to do a regular sweep to check out who is entering and leaving the bar. This is subconsciously noted as she mentally ticks the box marked 'philanderer'. Another babe walks by with hardly any clothes on – keep listening and looking at the babe you're talking to. She will be mightily impressed and mentally tick the box marked 'He's Mine'.

Mirroring

This is the process of copying what she is doing – if she leans forward you lean forward, if she puts her hand up to her chin, you do the same. We all tend to do this subconsciously as a rule anyway, but you can emphasise it slightly and boost the effect. Don't overdo it though, or else she'll think she's playing a game of 'Simon says'.

Encroach on her space

We all have an invisible comfort zone of space between ourselves and the next person, whether they be a friend or stranger, which changes with circumstance (e.g. squeezed together at Oxford Circus underground station) or mood (during the course of a date). You generally start off apart and move closer together as her defences soften. Once you're inside her 'private exclusion zone' you have been accepted into her inner circle. Take this as a sign that you are getting warm.

Touching

It's OK to touch, but don't try and put your hand up her skirt the minute she moves towards you. The trick is gentle and frequent brushing of her skin with your hand on her arm or shoulder. But don't pat her – she's not a dog (well, we hope not) and she doesn't need winding. Women hate being patted. Move a strand of her hair out of her face, or touch her arm. She should like that.

Lean closer

Once you're inside her personal exclusion zone, whisper something to her – anything – whether it be a compliment, a secret or just because the bar or restaurant is too loud, but whisper something. Once you've got your hot wet lips gently brushing against her ear, you should see some rapid forward movement, through the next stage and on to the big one – kissing.

> **TIP:** *Note the phrase 'gently brushing' and resist the temptation to stick your tongue in her ear or bite her lobes. That comes later.*

Moving in for the kiss

That first kiss is a monumentally important one. I don't mean that social butterfly, cheek-to-cheek kiss that you give when you first meet or disappear after a first date. I mean *that* kiss, the one that says: this is it, we're serious, Game On! The first kiss is the starting point of the whole proceedings and is the physical foundation stone of what is to follow. That first kiss is a bridgehead, a physical display of you both surrendering your defences and a tangible measure of your desire for one another.

I was watching a documentary on TV about prostitutes the other night and one of the girls interviewed said that she would never kiss a client. It's remarkable that a prostitute will have oral sex, anal sex, full sex and golden showers with a complete stranger for money but will refuse to kiss them, because she considers kissing far more 'intimate' than sexual intercourse.

Never underestimate the importance of that first kiss. Yes, I know schoolgirls will run around a party saying, 'I've snogged Jim' and 'I've snogged Steve' – who cares? What we're talking about here is real women. Your *right woman, right now* woman for whom this first kiss is very important indeed.

How do you know when it's the right time? You just do. Most couples have a mental blackout during those crucial micro-seconds between the lean forward and the lip squishing. How did it happen? It just does. Once you get *that* close it's an inevitable consequence.

First-kiss technique

- **How deep should you go?** Tongues should be part of the equation, but don't try and lick her tonsils.

- **To be continued.** Back off and say something sweet like, 'That was amazing' or 'I enjoyed that', before going back for another one. Whatever you do, don't interpret this as a sign to go free for all. Avoid the temptation to try and stick your hands up her dress and down her front two seconds after the first kiss. Savour the moment like a fine wine and let your hormonal power surge calm down. There's still a long way to go.

> **TIP:** *Always leave a woman wanting more, not trying to fight you off to stop you from getting more.*

How to say soppy stuff to women (which they love) without sounding like a twat

There's a knack to whispering sweet nothings to women without coming over as if you've been rehearsing it for ten years. One of the reasons foreign men always go down so well with home-grown 'lasses' is that, because their command of the English language is so crap, they get away with being incredibly blunt and direct.

I've seen it a thousand times from my first school trip to Paris, to the Club Med in Jamaica. Some swarthy Latino hunk has got the attention of Princess No.1 and is saying, 'Zou haf ze mist bootifuel eyze. I sink I lurve you.' And they fall for it every time. The thing is they are saying precisely what she wants to hear and they are lapping it up. About a million years ago Rick Astley had a hit singing: 'I'll never let you down, I'll be there whenever you need me.' That's what women want to hear yet we Brits are so stiff-upper-lipped we need a gun at our head before we say three little words like 'I love you', and rarely deliver them in a dignified or credible manner. By the time we've mustered the courage, energy and chutzpah to get the words out it sounds so trite and rehearsed it loses any impact.

To be fair, our girls are much more forgiving of foreign men and half dismiss British men before we open our mouths. Yet, clever guys know the value attached to saying the right thing at the right time, and will unashamedly and expertly pepper their language with the odd 'keynote phrase' that makes a woman go all gooey and weak.

TIP: *Try and say something meaningful when they least expect it – it carries more impact. (But not when she's driving you on a windy, unlit country road at night. She'll be so shocked she'll drive into a tree.) Keep it simple and make every word count. When you say it, reach out and touch a part of her – a hand, arm or shoulder, and don't gush.*

- 'I think we've got something special going here. I can really feel it.'

- 'I've never met a woman who made me feel as good as you do. Thank you.'

- 'These last few weeks since we've been together have been awesome.'

- 'I hope you're as ecstatic with me as I am with you.'

Get the intonation and the delivery right and once you've said it, you'll have to have her surgically removed from your body. Have a tissue handy because she *will* get a tear in her eye. If you add something like, 'Well, I think so anyway' or 'What do you think?' she will counter you and say something equally sensual.

Don't have sex

A clever strategy to adopt, especially with a woman who is emotionally bruised after having come out of a bad relationship, or after having been dumped or emotionally roughed up, is to suggest that you sleep together, but you won't attempt any kind of sex for two weeks or a month. This is what we call a noble gesture. She'll think it novel and cute and it builds instant trust. Of course, it really is only a *gesture*.

Once you've established that you are not going to do anything you can torment her half to death by describing – in detail – what you would like to do to her when you finally reach the deadline, when the game goes *live*.

However, I'd be surprised if you last the full course. I've tried this several times and we didn't last a week without ripping into each other. Once you are in a bed together, after a couple of nights of righteous high-octane cuddling, pecks on the cheek and platonic petting, you'll probably find she will be leaping on you with passion and enthusiasm or pleading with you to do the same.

If you do actually make it to the agreed date without sex, make the sex night into a special occasion. Think of it as a wedding night. She'll appreciate it and remember it.

Seven things to notice about a woman to get brownie points

A woman is a changeable feast and throughout the month will go through more costume changes than Madonna. There are seven key things about herself that she changes radically every five minutes and if you can tune yourself into these seven things you will score huge brownie points and seriously go up in her estimation. I know you're not interested in any of them – you couldn't care whether or not she's wearing La Perla underwear or Gossard, as long as you can get your hands on her breasts. My argument is that the more you notice these girlie items and let her know you've noticed, the more brownie points you get and the more frequently you touch the breasts. Get it? Think of it as air miles on toast.

1. **Her hair.** A woman's hair is her crowning glory and the litmus paper by which she judges everything else. If she

has a terrific style and sharp cut, it looks great and is clean and shiny, then she's on top of the world. If it's dirty or she's got split ends and hasn't had a decent cut for months and can't decide whether to grow it out or get it cut short then she's bound to be moody and irritable and a right pain in the ass.

You can score big here by recognising her problem and suggesting a solution: 'I know this stylist who just worked with *Vogue* on a shoot. I'll book you an appointment.' Or you could at least notice when it's going well: 'Your hair looks awesome.'

> **TIP:** *Never ask a woman how much she's spent on having it done. If you thought your wash, cut and restyle at Toni & Guy was off the chart she's just spent the equivalent of a round-the-world air ticket.*

2. **Her weight.** Have you ever heard a woman *not* discuss her weight gain or loss during the course of a day? Or weigh up the merits of another piece of cheesecake? All women are obsessed with their weight. Obsessed. Generally women put weight on very quickly (notice that the weight never goes on anywhere where it doesn't matter) and lose weight painfully slowly. However, when they do, you need to notice (even if it is the tiniest amount), particularly if they are trying out some new diet or pill.

Best way of dealing with this is to anticipate the inevitable question – 'Do I look big in this?' or 'Do you think my bottom is fat?' – by going on a pre-emptive strike. Simply look at her semi-quizzically, but in an approving manner, and say something like, 'Babe, have you lost weight?' She won't give you the pleasure of knowing, but she is now the happiest woman on the planet.

3. **Her clothes.** She's probably spent about five hours shopping for the right outfit she deemed appropriate to wear for you on your first date, so the least you can do is notice. Confident older women often have a set look that they casually slip into for the ritual of coupling; younger or unconfident women generally try a variety of outfits, so don't be shocked if she seems to be trying slightly too hard or making an exhibition of herself. 'No, those pink, thigh-high boots are very fetching – they match the neon-orange floral top remarkably well.'

4. **Her handbag.** A woman's handbag is the equivalent of a man's car, and is a huge status symbol. She will probably have one for every occasion, although not quite every minute of the day. 'Fantastic handbag' is all you need say. Avoid the temptation to add, 'Can I put my car keys, mobile phone, iPod and wallet in there?'

5. **Her shoes.** You must have heard of Imelda Marcos, the wife of the fallen Philippine dictator, who was found to have over 5,000 pairs of shoes in her wardrobe while the masses starved to death. All women are closet Imeldas and their hunger for a pair of Manola Blahnik pumps or Jimmy Shoo dress shoes knows no bounds. No matter how gorgeous or well endowed your date is, don't forget to look down at her feet when you meet. The correct response is: 'Wow, babe, those shoes are awesome.' Or words to that effect.

6. **Her earrings.** You probably wonder why, if a woman has only one pair of ears, she has 6,000 pairs of earrings. Don't ask, it's a complete mystery. Just accept that women will buy at least one new pair of earrings a month, or a week, and look out for their appearance. A casual 'Great

earrings – are they white gold or platinum?' or 'Are they tanzanite?' will make her feel like a million dollars. Not only did you notice she was wearing them, and that they were *new*, but you had some inkling of what they were made of. Full marks.

7. **Her shade of lipstick/make-up.** Women are masters of disguise in that they can radically change their look with the stroke of an eye-liner pencil. When you pitch up to take her out she can either look like an extra from the Addams Family, a peaches-and-cream farm girl or somewhere in the middle. Some women get this unbelievably right and always look terrific, but other women can get it so very wrong. Never ever look surprised when she arrives in black lipstick and thick purple blusher. Take it in your stride. Just order food in and get a video.

    Most women settle down to one kind of look or another and certainly by the age of 28, they should have decided what 'look' suits them best. However, depending on what colours Estée Lauder or Chanel deem 'in' this season will determine what colours she turns up in and the 'in' colours don't always work. When she's just spent 10 quid on a lipstick and 15 quid on nail polish and eye-liner, it's advisable to mention that. 'That Frosty Pink looks fabulous – it really suits you.' Don't say, 'Urgh, what's that gunge on your lips?'

9
Sex

Be a great lover, tonight

The right attitude

Being a great lover is 80 per cent inspiration and 20 per cent perspiration, so first work on your head. Great lovers are not selfish, pushy, boastful, sexist, ignorant or inhibited. Great lovers are honest, modest, fun, intelligent, experimental, relaxed, caring and measured. The trick is to be vulnerable without being a wimp. Vulnerable means you are open to suggestion and new ideas, which she will quickly translate as sensitive to her needs. Being a wimp is simply being a pathetic loser, which she will translate into yesterday's man. Rev your ego by doing a mental stocktake of your strong points. You're a good-looking boy and your body isn't half bad for your age.

You've got a decent job, you dress well, your place looks suitably hip and you're a nice guy. Hey, she should be paying you. You are terrific and deserve to be right here with your right woman, right now.

> **TIP:** *If none of the above is true then you'd better put in a spot of spadework.*

Talk the talk

Remember: foreplay for women starts about a week before we men think it does. Try calling her, texting her or e-mailing her throughout the day and tease her with sexy thoughts ranging from 'I can't wait to see you' to 'You make me feel so horny I can't concentrate on my work.' If you know her well, you might try 'Tonight I'm going to tie you up, smother you in low-fat strawberry yoghurt and slowly lick it off.'

During the pre-sex warm-up, talk dirty to her. This does not mean a barrage of four-letter words. Be clever not crude. Set her mind alight and her imagination racing. Tell her what you would like to do to her. Ask her if there is anything she would like to have done to her, or something she has never tried but would like to. The less inhibited and more comfortable you make her feel, the better she – and you – will perform. When in an intimate situation ask open-ended questions that don't elicit a yes/no answer. Instead ask, 'How does it feel when I do this?' or 'When I stroke you here is it better like this, or this?' If you're intimate in conversation, she'll be intimate in bed.

Keep it real

Don't pretend that you know everything if you quite clearly don't. Always be honest. It's better to say, 'I've never tried that before but I can't wait to give it a whirl.' But don't be so serious that you forget to have fun. We all take sex far too seriously. Inject a bit of laughter into the proceedings. Let's face it, a grown man and woman getting naked, feeling each other all over and rubbing their bits together until one makes a mess is a pretty hilarious concept. Forget about being good in bed – aim to be bad in bed. Sex should be sweaty and primitive, filthy and disgusting – not neat and clinical. After sex your bedroom should look like post-World War III Baghdad, and at least one item of furniture should be smashed. If your duvet remains uncreased we need to talk.

Don't be afraid to fail. If you try something new or radical or physically challenging, then if it doesn't work or it's painful or uncomfortable, stop and try something else. It matters but not a lot. You can create a game situation where you both take turns to suggest something you've always wanted to try.

Set the right mood

You've heard this before but it's worth repeating because it's so obvious: we all forget or ignore the basics. You may find the one woman who loves having sex on the back of your motorbike in the company car park in a force 10 gale, but most women prefer to make love in comfortable surroundings. This means:

• **Shelter.** To be a great lover you need to exert the territorial advantage. If you haven't got a great place of your own either borrow one or rent one. Hotel rooms are a magical aphrodisiac. Preferably somewhere that has a certain style and cache and certainly not any hotel that rents rooms by the hour.

• **Warmth.** If your pad feels like a mortuary, turn the heater on, you skinflint. She'll never take her clothes off if she already has blue lips and goose bumps. For sex, the room temperature should be the same as that inside a Kew Gardens greenhouse. Always assuming you're not actually doing it in a Kew Gardens greenhouse.

- **Fresh flowers.** Buy some dramatic fresh flowers like arum lilies (those long-stemmed white flutes) and stick them in a vase – or two or three. You can never have enough flowers.

- **A gift.** As a surprise, buy her a small expression of your love, expertly wrapped in decent paper, not handed to her in a brown paper bag. It could be a box of Bendicks mints, a candle or, if you're a flash git, an air ticket to New York (don't forget to buy yourself one as well!). The value is in the gesture and the unwrapping. It makes her feel special. Women love unwrapping anything.

- **Candles.** Don't ask me why but women go bananas for candles. Big ones, long ones, fat ones, thin ones … even tiny little tea candles. Candles make women go all gooey and romantic. Buy a load and light them all over the flat. Especially in the bathroom. Scented ones work even better.

- **Crisp, clean linen.** Throw out those disgusting sticky green polyester sheets you had at university, and haven't washed since. Get to John Lewis or Marks & Spencer and treat yourself to a decent set of white bed linen.

- **Music.** If she's into jazz try Ella Fitzgerald, Duke Ellington or Nina Simone; more funky try Marvin Gaye, the Alan Parsons Project. Vibey Jamiroqua. Ethereal Enya or … better still, ask her to choose the music while you pour the drinks, knowing that you have an eclectic collection and she should find something she likes.

- **Booze.** A decent bottle of Chardonnay or Cabernet Sauvignon (definitely nothing out of a box) should slip down a treat. Lining up a row of shot glasses with B-52s or tequila and chanting 'Down in one' is very déclassé unless you've just come back from a friend's wedding and you're both equally hammered.

- **A video camera.** There's something ferociously exciting about starring in your own blue movie – for her and for you. But before you whip out your multi-focus Sony handycam, there are a few ground rules. Reassure her that she can keep the film if she likes and if she doesn't then you will not show it to anybody else.

Make her feel good about herself

She only feels as good as you make her feel. So if you sit there talking about the weather she's not going to be overly impressed. Tell her how fantastic she looks, how sexy her dress is, how you've fantasised about feeling her body and kissing her breasts for the past six months. If it isn't true, lie. It won't be the first time that a few well-chosen white lies will have smoothed the passage of seduction.

I'm not worthy, I'm not worthy – last-minute pre-sex panics

Look, pal, she's with you. She wouldn't be there if she didn't want to be. She laughed at your jokes heartily. She caressed your arm lovingly. She kissed you enthusiastically. Now she's in your bedroom making herself very comfortable on your fresh Irish linen. There are approximately 30 million other British males who would kill to be in your position, right now. She has decided on you. Refresh her glass of Chardonnay and get on with it. Hurry along now.

Timing is everything

I remember watching a sex education video at school featuring two lusty locusts. Boy locust walked around girl locust a couple of times and then leapt on her back and started prodding about like a maniac. Boy locust didn't take girl locust to the movies, indulge in meaningful conversation or even buy her a coffee. This is *not*, repeat *not*, the way to do it and, frankly, is a bad example to be showing a class of impressionable nine-year-olds. Know this: women can react pretty violently when they're leapt on when they're not quite ready to be leapt on.

Seven sure signs of readiness

1. **Her face is flushed** like she's just completed the London Marathon.

2. **Her body temperature is so high** you could fry an egg on the back of her neck.

3. **Her lips are full** and red and wet and she is kissing you feverishly.

4. **Her clothes** are all on the floor.

5. **She is humping** your leg like next door's Jack Russell.

6. **She's speechless** because she has your favourite anatomical part in her mouth.

7. **She's screaming** 'Take me now, big boy' or similar. And I mean screaming.

Four sure signs of non-readiness

1. **She is still wearing her overcoat.** This means she does not feel at all comfortable with the situation. It may need some simple remedy like turning the heating up or getting rid of that cockroach in the kitchen. Or she might have just found out that you slept with her best friend, in which case either you or she had better leave.

2. **She is not wet,** or at least damp, anywhere on her body. Either she's not interested, or severely frightened or inhibited, or both. Some women never get wet in the appropriate target zone – never – which is why they invented KY jelly and saliva. Avoid using that stinky synthetic body lotion from the flea market as a lubricant or her vagina could sting for the next fortnight. You might want to try lying her down gently and administering ten minutes of quality oral sex instead.

3. **You're doubled up** on the ground with your testicles where your eyeballs used to be. Whatever you said or did she certainly did not approve of at this moment in time. Back off and try again later – like in about six months. What was it she took exception to anyway?

4. **She has left the building.** OK guys, it's back to the drawing board with this one. Where did the evening start going wrong? Was it something you said? Or was it that T-shirt with the slogan WOMEN ARE ONLY GOOD FOR ONE THING plastered across your chest? It's worth analysing what went wrong with a 'promising' evening and pinpointing the crucial moment when it turned against you. Why did she do that? Be honest now.

Assuming she is ready, now get down to business

Whoa boy! Take your time. What's the hurry? Sex is not a race. We've all heard the jokes about the guy whose lovemaking lasts less than a minute. Don't let this be you. Savour each moment like it is a mouthful of vintage champagne, every kiss as if it were your last. You want to caress and squeeze, nibble and tease and extend the experience, making it last as long as possible and not turn it into a wham-bam-thank-you-mam disappointment.

Foreplay

As mentioned earlier, foreplay started when you first called her this morning. Now it's getting serious. She needs to be kissed properly on the lips. Kissing gives a woman the emotional closeness she craves. Her lips, tongue and mouth are some of the most erogenous parts of her body. Stimulating kissing will arouse her whole body. Take your time and vary the pressure, duration and location. Use your hands to hold her and caress her whole body.

By now she should be reaching the point where her body shows physical signs of desire and she's probably as horny as you thought you were. Her breasts will swell, her nipples will harden, her breath will quicken, her eyes will widen (that's why they call them bedroom eyes) and her labia will swell and become moist. In the ensuing carnage both your clothes should have been suitably ripped off.

Oral sex

A survey showed that over 50 per cent of British women have never experienced oral sex, i.e. having it done to them. It's time to redress the balance of statistics. Don't wait for her, follow her body down from her neck to her breasts to her stomach to her labia and lose yourself in her folds of flesh. Her reaction should be explosive. Women often get a twinge of self-doubt – about how she smells and tastes – so a little encouragement ('You taste divine') will go a long way.

The biggie
To be a great lover (in her eyes) you need to give her pleasure and the woman-on-top position is notorious for allowing her to grind away to orgasm. Touch her breasts, kiss her face and allow her to stimulate herself as well. In fact actively encourage her: 'Show me how you masturbate.' Orientals suggest nine shallow thrusts followed by one deep one but let's not get too scientific here. Try and almost reach orgasm and then back off. Maybe change position slightly and then build your momentum again. Variety and invention are more important than thrusting in and out for half an hour.

Orgasm
A woman's orgasm has as much to do with what's going on inside her head as what you're doing down below. They can almost get there several times before you push them over the edge and what stops a lot of women reaching orgasm is the pressure we put on them to have one. If it doesn't happen, keep practising. This is the time to talk to her and tell her how much she turns you on and how fantastic she looks and feels and ... whoops there she goes.

The follow-through
Like a good golf swing, you mustn't forget the follow-through. Before you roll over and start snoring, take time to hold her

tight, kiss her and compliment her. Resist the urge to be a cliché and ask how it was for her, or say something crude like, 'Christ, that was the shag of the century.' And don't thank her. She's not a charity. Instead say something neutral like, 'Wow, that was amazing.' You'll know how well you've done by her reaction. If she's trying to get her breath back and untangle one foot from behind her neck and the other from the bedstead, then it must have been good. If she's busy crocheting a tea cosy then you're out of luck.

Oh, by the way, if you're still feeling frisky, you can always start all over again – this time with slightly more feeling.

How to deal with her strange requests

When you give a woman the sexual reins then she will invariably come up with something interesting, imaginative and erotic that pushes your sexual envelope. Whatever it is, whether it be a spot of S&M, role-playing games (doctors and nurses, rich bitch and tradesman) or a simple request to kiss her properly, nine times out of ten it will be manageable – physically, emotionally and socially. Then she throws you a curved ball. Let's say she wants you to perform oral sex on her under the table in a restaurant. Heading down south in the middle of a prawn curry at the Bombay Duck does not go down (if you'll pardon the pun) well with the management. However, there are ways around it.

- **Fake it.** There is a company in the UK that makes a tidy profit recreating sexual fantasies for a bevy of uninhibited clients. But you can do the same at home. Set the table and the mood with a few candles and pretend you're at the restaurant, or wherever her fantasy scenario is set.

- **Talk it up.** Describe the action to her: you're on a train, surrounded by businessmen; you're in a restaurant and the handsome waiter/gorgeous waitress is watching; her useless ineffectual husband has left for work and you've surreptitiously crept into the family bed. Take your imagination anywhere it wants to go, and push your fantasies to the limit.

- **Use props.** A friend of mine went to the length of hiring a policeman's outfit for what he called the 'speeding fine' fantasy. He'd arrive on the doorstep in true 'Hello, hello, hello' fashion, ask to see her driving licence and admonish her for her tardy driving for a few minutes before she ripped off his uniform in search of his baton. He said the sex was mind-blowing.

So long as her request doesn't involve physical harm, public ridicule or arrest, then it's difficult to say 'no'. The trick, as with all sexual experimentation, is to attempt it, give it your best shot and if it doesn't work move on.

Psst! Don't ever talk about your sexual encounters to anyone else

Keep them secret and sacred. When you're very young it's a natural human instinct and virtually impossible not to brag to your mates that you've just performed kinky sex with the hottest babe on campus. This does not go down well when the hottest babe on campus finds out that you've been telling everybody about your intimate moments. This is when you fall out and she starts spreading the retaliatory rumour that you have a tiny penis, your body odour is suffocating and you were useless in bed.

As you get older you realise the power of silence and how

women truly respect the courtesy of having their private life remain private, and the thrill of the conspiracy that exists between you. Talk in broad strokes, if you have to – 'She's fantastic, a very sexy woman' – but never in graphic detail.

10
Be careful out there

Any man who spends time alone with a woman runs a risk. You can only gauge a woman's age, background, calibre and psychological behaviour pattern based on one or two fleeting meetings and although you may claim to be a good judge of character, you never know. She may be psychologically deranged, have had a string of STDs or simply hate men. There are three specific areas of concern where a man is vulnerable: 1) accusation of rape, 2) Aids and sex-related diseases, and 3) her falling pregnant.

Read on carefully.

Date rape

Only you and the woman know what really goes on between the two of you behind closed doors and should she, for any reason, want to hurt you then she is in a very powerful position. All she has to do is make one phone call to the police and cry 'rape' and your life, as you know it, is over. To avoid any confusion:

- **Don't force the issue.** The dilemma we men face is that, as documented earlier in this book, women often say a type of 'no' or 'I shouldn't' when what they mean is that they still want you to proceed. This is fine when you've still got your clothes on in a bar, but in the heat of a steamy session when you're half-undressed, the trick is knowing when that soft 'no' becomes a hard 'NO', and if you're in any sort of doubt, back off. If she then says, 'Why did you stop?' don't get into an open debate about 'I thought you didn't want to . . .', just kiss her and get back in the saddle immediately.

- **A woman can say 'no'** at any time during the proceedings, including the moment of penetration, for whatever reason, and should this happen, the right move is to respect this, back off and calm down. If you can, leave the building.

If you are wrongly accused

There have been so many false accusations of rape and sexual harassment recently that there is a movement afoot to establish laws that penalise those women who use this strategy of wrongful accusation for whatever reason. Apart from the damage to the man concerned in every aspect of his life, false accusations undermine the cases of those women who genuinely are raped and legitimately have a case.

- The police and forensic scientists have very sophisticated methods of determining whether or not a coupling was in fact rape or not. So even if you've had intercourse, if you didn't rape her, then there is a slim (but only *very* slim) chance that the evidence will bear you out. But this is *not* enough.

- The press are full of stories of men who have been wrongfully accused of rape by a woman for various reasons – they were scorned, or they couldn't admit to having an affair and cried 'rape' to ease the guilt. Whatever the motive, the bottom line is this: even if you are vindicated and it is proven beyond a shadow of a doubt that you did not rape a woman, once you have been accused of rape, your reputation is permanently damaged.

- Rough or bully-boy sex is not rape, although it could be construed as rape if the woman changes her mind halfway through. The same rules apply whatever the type of sex. It is particularly difficult if you are role-playing or in the middle of some S&M game, where the possibility of misinterpreting the signals when her succession of no's are part of the script is a mind-blow. Here it is suggested to use a trigger word or phrase, let's say 'Tony Blair', which means stop right now, put your clothes back on and go home.

Aids and sexual responsibility

The whole Aids pandemic has created an air of caution among the singles community and the authorities and it is something to take seriously and protect yourself against as much as you can. The basic rule of thumb is always use a condom whoever you're with and whatever the circumstance. As we agreed earlier, before you meet your *right woman* you will meet many wrong women and the fact that you need to try out a good number of relationships before you meet your *right woman* is counter to what the World Health Organisation would like, i.e. have sex once with one partner, get married and settle down. It doesn't work like that.

Remember, though, that these days it is not done to be seen as a 'player', a 'Romeo' or a 'philanderer', or any of those other derogatory terms, and publicly parade your 'sexual conquests'. So if you consider yourself a sexual conquistador or have ever collected the 'panties' of the women you've slept with, or carved notches into your bedhead, then this is the time to stop. That is very déclassé. You are merely your average guy trying to get ahead with women and find the right one for you. The quieter you keep any rogue male behaviour, the better you will fare.

But don't forget to take precautions

Use a condom – it isn't clever to ignore the warnings and avoid using a condom, especially in the early days of a relationship. I'd be surprised if any smart modern-thinking woman would allow you to have full sex with her without one these days, even if she is on the pill or using some other form of contraception. Wearing a condom sends her a message that you care enough to protect her, the inference being that if you need to protect yourself then you must have something to protect and therefore are not infected. If you're worried about the fact that casually slipping a condom out of your wallet means she'll think you're a complete womaniser, then explain that you've had the condom for ages and feel it is the right thing to do.

Wearing a condom is not an insult to her; you're not subliminally sending a message that she might be infected.

For those guys for whom the thought of wearing a condom always makes them go limp, and it is a fact that for some men, condom-wearing leads to major erection loss, there are a couple of techniques you can employ to successfully stay hard:

- **Let her do it.** If you incorporate the putting on of the condom into the act of foreplay and give her the active role of rolling it down the length of your penis, then this is a very erotic act and the chances are you will stay hard.

- **Make sure the condom is handy,** i.e. wrapper ripped down the side and left under the pillow. If you have to run downstairs to get one from the glove compartment of your car in your Y-fronts, then the moment is lost. And you can kiss goodbye to your erection.

The pregnancy trap

OK, here's a scenario you might want to be very wary of. Many women, especially those in a wobbly relationship, think that to get pregnant is one way of cementing your allegiance to her – thinking that everything will be all right when the baby arrives. One man told of his nightmare with one woman who he had sex with on only two occasions using a condom. He really liked the woman but didn't see her as a long-term prospect, and certainly didn't see her as the mother of his children, but their relationship was fun and convenient. After the second coupling together she called him two weeks later and said that she thought she was pregnant. Impossible, he thought, since he knew he was wearing a condom. After much mental argy-bargy and a thorough medical it transpired that she was indeed pregnant – she later confessed to squeezing the sperm out of the condom and emptying it into her vagina, knowing that she was at her most fertile.

> **Tip:** *When using a condom, when you finish always tie a knot in it and dispose of it yourself.*

The baby desperado

There are some women out there who are desperate to have a child of their own, even if it means being a single mother – and they could feasibly trap you into getting them pregnant without you knowing. Their noble plan, at the outset, is to bring up the child on their own without your involvement in the child-rearing. This is all very well and something that you are oblivious to, if all goes according to plan, until the bills mount up and you suddenly get a letter from her lawyer out of the blue – always when you've just found your *right woman* – demanding maintenance (which usually ends in a court case where you are made to look like the neglectful, uncaring slob who got her pregnant). Which can not only be expensive, but is incredibly embarrassing and is always awkward timing. There is never a good time to get the news that you owe money on a child you didn't know you had. Be careful out there.

Men's problems – it's a guy thing

Losing it

There isn't a man on the planet who can put his hand on his heart and say that he has never ever lost an erection whether it was at a crucial moment or not. It happens, and it happens to just about everybody, even porn stars. If you've always enjoyed a great sex life, adore your partner and thought your tackle was in full working order, this erection loss can be a vein-opening experience if you let it get to you. No, you're not impotent – for most men this is just a temporary malfunction and normal service will be resumed as soon as humanly possible. There are many reasons why you just lost it.

The fear factor

The reason men are prone to losing it is, anthropologists tell us, because the need to be ready to fight is ingrained deep within our psyche. Picture this: you're on the job with Mrs Cavewoman when a sabre-toothed tiger comes roaring into the mouth of the cave. Now you don't want to be facing off a tiger while sporting *erecticus giganticus* so our Maker, in His infinite wisdom, made the penis downsize at the slightest hint of fear.

True story

I once had an affair with a woman who was married. She used to come down to my place in London and we'd share wild times. Then one night she invited me down to her place in Hereford. She met me at the railway station, we had a delightful meal at a local restaurant and then went back to her place to do the hokey-cokey. One look at the family photos on the sideboard and my spine turned to custard. She'd conveniently omitted to tell me that her husband was in the SAS. He looked as if he could give you an instant tonsillectomy with his thumb and first finger.

'Don't worry,' she said, sensing my discomfort, 'he's on night exercise, or whatever, this week.' An hour later, after a couple of drinks of *his* Cabernet Sauvignon, I'd relaxed and the desire to get hold of her magnificent breasts overtook my fear of going without tonsils. We were right in the middle of things when she said, innocently, 'Sometimes Derek pops in to collect some things during the night. But don't worry, he never comes upstairs.'

Hello, was she completely insane? My penis was deflated, packed and out of the house before I had time to get dressed. Fear is the biggest governing factor on a penis's turgidity, although today the fear of tigers has been replaced by fear of the sack, rejection and financial ruin. Collectively this fear is known as 'stress'.

Stress
Stress is the biggest killer in the world. It's the invisible worry factor that haunts your mind when you least expect it and is currently billed by the World Health Organisation as a major debilitating factor in sexual dysfunction. Let's suppose you run your own business and one of your suppliers is threatening to liquidate you unless you find £100,000 by Friday – the fact that you are even attempting sex is a miracle. Or if you're an employee, hands all over her body, and hers on yours, when her expression reminds you of Tracey at work ... which reminds you that you forgot to tell Tracey to deliver the disk with the company annual report on to the printers ... and if you don't get it to Milton Keynes by 4 p.m. tomorrow you're history.

And you wonder where your erection went?

Too physically ambitious
You might well have read about this 'ancient Chinese position' that has given exquisite pleasure to a harem of Lotus Blossoms, where, if she bends over the photocopier and you slide down the banister at precisely 24 miles per hour with a 24-degree angle of dangle, then you can get far deeper penetration than you ever thought possible. Exotic new positions are fantastic and all very well but sometimes you can be

overly ambitious in the new-position stakes and practically wrench the head off your penis in an attempt to follow the 'ancient Chinese love manual' to the letter. The trick is to get hard and slip your rock-hard penis inside her, get your confidence up and then, and only then, start messing about with the fancy stuff. If you find yourself trying to enter a woman while turning the pages of a 'How to' book, throw the book away. Use your natural basic instinct – it's worked for about 4 million years.

Too eager

If you try and make love before she is ready, i.e. suitably lubricated, then it is painful for both you and her, and it feels as if you're sticking your penis into a tube of broken glass. Remember, your penis is a yellow-bellied coward and as soon as it starts feeling the slightest pain it retreats to safer climes. Think what happens when you go swimming in ice-cold water – your trusty length of salami shrinks to the size of an acorn.

If you stumble at the first attempt, relax and slowly start your build-up again. Once things start going badly and you actively begin to think about getting an erection, then no matter how many Eiffel Towers you construct, or falling chimney stacks you reverse, you won't get one. Think instead about how beautiful, adorable and desirable she is. Concentrate on her body and her smells and flashbacks of past successes to get your arousal going. This is not the time to switch to the porn channel. She will take this as a serious slight on her potency as a female and question your motives.

> **TIP:** *If she's having a dry spell – and many women over thirty-five do – you might want to use saliva to help her along. Just trickle a layer of spit on your middle finger and*

apply to her vagina without her knowing. Once she feels herself getting wet, she will start getting wetter – which is exactly the same as men. Research shows that once we actively see ourselves getting hard, we get harder. So don't stop looking at your penis and always make love with the lights on.

Mind games

Sometimes her body language sends out confusing signals and you're not sure whether she wants to make love or not. Something she does, sometimes even her tone of voice, makes you feel that she's just going through the motions on automatic, which is a total passion killer in itself. In which case back off and try again later. If you're in an advanced state of readiness, your hand is in her knickers, your mouth is around her nipple and she says, 'Dahling, do you think the orchids look better in the dining room or the bedroom?' you can accurately deduce that she's not that interested in sex at this moment in time.

Talk about it

When loss of erection happens, don't try and make a joke about it. It isn't *that* serious, but it isn't *that* funny either. And don't turn on your side with your back to her and go to sleep without saying anything and pretending that what just didn't happen, didn't really happen. As we boys all know, the penis has a complete mind of its own – sometimes you can't keep the damn thing down and sometimes it just doesn't feel like playing ball. It is a mystery. Don't try and explain away the unexplainable. Say something like, 'Well, babe, I don't know what the hell's going on down there but maybe we can try again later. My penis is being a lazy bastard, sorry.'

Women are very understanding and can be uncharacteristically generous at such a time. However, given that when a woman is geared up for a hot session, and she's expecting you to deliver one, then she is bound to be severely disappointed when you don't. Believe me, it may be the first time it has happened to you but it sure won't be the first time it's happened to her. She will worry that you don't find her attractive enough, that this is a chronic problem and she's destined for a lifetime of sexless romance or Viagra-popping mayhem. Reassure her that none of the above is true, that you find her unbelievably attractive and that you will be back in the saddle as soon as you've had eight hours sleep and a bowl of cornflakes.

Premature ejaculation

Premature ejaculation usually means an ejaculation during foreplay or during penetration before any serious stroke-work has begun. It's interesting that the politics of sex has reached a stage where if you make a woman orgasm early on, then you are a hero, but if you ejaculate early on you are considered an unskilled and inconsiderate lover. This is because women have the potential for multiple orgasms, whereas we poor saps generally ejaculate once, the sleep hormone kicks in and we need those aforementioned eight hours of sleep and three Shredded Wheat before we're ready to go again.

Consequently, if you want to be considered a great lover, and prolong the session, it's good etiquette to get her to reach at least one orgasm and get that in the bag before you get really started. Even the Karma Sutra suggests that you ideally give a woman an orgasm before you enter her, if you can – always assuming that she can. Some women claim not to be able to reach orgasm unless they have full-on penetrative sex. You can spend a good hour or so of blissful experimentation with her body trying to prove her wrong. Research shows that the average sex session lasts a dismal four minutes, so anything under that is a major problem.

Sexologists I've spoken to claim that the incidence of this ailment is increasing. However, although premature ejaculation is considered a depressingly bleak problem by those who suffer from it, there are numerous tried-and-tested techniques that can overcome the problem quickly and painlessly.

> **TIP:** *The trick with any of these sexual problems is to talk to the right expert sooner rather than later. Your doctor is the best starting point and he will advise a specialist, but if you live in a small town where you bump into the doctor at the pub, you might want to try the nearest big city's sex clinic where your anonymity will be guaranteed.*

11
Auxiliary skills

Starfucking

You can spend your life chasing a fantasy that exists only in your head, which is where, in nine times out of ten, it should stay. We've all watched videos of Britney Spears in bobby socks and Kylie Minogue waving her choice butt around, licked our lips and thought, 'Mm, wouldn't it be great to give her one over the sofa.' It's a natural instinct and it's healthy. Britney and Kylie couldn't care less what you think; in fact, they actively want you to think that. It is the required and pre-dicted effect. Sex sells and that's why Kylie and Britney have just sold 20 million albums between them.

But the chances of you rogering Britney, Kylie and a verit-able harem of gorgeous celebrity tottie are very slim indeed –

unless (and this is a BIG unless) you get close to them, and I don't mean hiding in the dustbin outside their mews cottage, which is commonly called stalking.

Get closer to them

If you want to get close to a celebrity, pursue a career that gets you close. Once you're in the film, music or fashion industry at a senior level, where you have some clout and can be of assistance to their career, you're suddenly surrounded by gorgeous wannabes and are an attractive proposition. It's far more powerful to say, 'I'm casting for the female lead opposite Russell Crowe in my latest romantic thriller. Are you interested?' than breathlessly gushing, 'I've seen all your films and think you're wonderful. Could you sign the back of my hand, please? Promise I'll never wash it off.'

There are plenty of opportunities to get near celebrities if you have a legal or financial background (particularly a divorce lawyer), or are a top celebrity PR agent or journalist. The trick is to get on the same, or similar, level as the celebrity, then there's no argument, which means not asking for her autograph on your first date.

The good news

Every woman celebrity I've ever interviewed has said practically the same thing, which boils down to: 'Men never approach me because I'm famous and they feel intimidated by my fame.' Yet invariably their roots are humble and underneath the glitter there is a loosely veiled plea to reconnect with those roots.

With celebrities you need to catch them when they are either on their way up or on their way down. That way you have something to offer. When they are at the top of their game they are seemingly aloof and arrogant because they will only mix with like people, i.e. other celebrities at the top of their game. It is a rarified club to which most mortals aren't usually invited.

Also consider this, the celebrity lifestyle is prohibitively expensive – they have to fly first class, eat at the best restaurants, be driven by limo, hire a bodyguard, and there is always an attendant entourage and bevy of hangers-on. A cheap uneventful day in the life of even the most modest A-list celebrity will cost about five to ten thousand quid. Could you really afford to keep up? The trick is to know your limits.

Why you don't really need a supermodel in your life

Do you really want to go out with a supermodel for any other reason than to boast to your mates? Let me tell you about fantasy women. You want to go out with a supermodel but believe me, you're not missing much if you don't. The reality is, they are never at home longer than a night at a time, and when they are they are so exhausted all they want to do is sleep; which means none of the mind-blowing, blue-movie sex you fantasised about having when watching her parade down the ramp in skimpy lingerie. Everywhere they go there's an army of photographers, models, designers, publicists, merchant bankers, party organisers and general hangers-on who would all kill their grannies to spend just one night inside her pants.

Consequently you will spend many a lonely night in your Clapham flat working out the time difference between London and New York, Milan and Tokyo and clocking up a hefty phone bill just to whisper your sweet nothings to deaf ears. All the time worrying why she didn't get back to her hotel room exactly when she said she would, and if Luigi, that hot new fashion photographer who looks like a dashing Argentine polo player, is, as we speak, wining, dining and shagging her. The bastard.

> **TIP:** *A babe has to be manageable otherwise she will drive you insane.*

How to talk dirty to a woman in a way she will enjoy

Most men feel that talking to a woman is a bit of an effort and that he is duty-bound to say something nice to her. Empty compliments like, 'Gosh, you're beautiful', delivered in an unemotional way like BT's speaking clock, will not get you very far. Yet what you say, and the speech patterns and words that you use, are an incredibly effective vehicle for seduction. Talking is a turn-on and what you say about her, how you describe what you desire to do to her and what you're actually doing while you're doing it, will leave a woman speechless. If radio is the theatre of the mind you should be the theatre of her mind.

Not all women will warm to talking dirty, but the majority of women do love being spoken to sexily and the simple act of communication makes them feel warmer towards you. They will view you as more confident, more honest and open.

If you're not very forthcoming in the verbal department outside the bedroom then you will probably find difficulty saying anything in the bedroom, but give it a try. It all depends on your background and how much or how little you've spoken throughout your life. Same goes for her.

Those of you who still feel inhibited or shy about talking about sex or simply giving suggestive compliments, get over it. Move on. Let yourself go. You need to release the power of your verbal skill. There are millions of men out there who never say a word from start to finish; they might argue that they don't *need* to talk, as they let their *actions* do the talking – but they are missing a trick. Word play is an aphrodisiac – it's seductive in itself. Try it.

News night

Think of it like the 6 o'clock news – as soon as the catchy signature tune is out of the way the first thing they do is tell you what they are about to tell you, during the main body of the newscast they tell you what they need to tell you and then, when wrapping up, they tell you what they've just told you. Apply this same technique to your seduction repertoire and you will achieve astounding results.

> **TIP:** *The trick is to be romantic, suggestive, blunt and explicit without being crass and vulgar. It can be done.*

Ease into it

She may have never been talked to during sex before and you may need to ease her into it. But once she gets used to the idea ... Wow! Say things like:

- 'Your breasts are magnificent; I could suck them all night.'

- 'I want to put my fingers inside your knickers and feel you getting wet.'

- 'Whenever I see a hint of your cleavage, you give me an instant hard-on.'

- 'You turn me on so much I can hardly breathe.'

- 'I don't think you realise how sexy you are.'

Match the talk to the moment

Such is the flexibility of talk that it performs a mixture of different functions. You can be:

- **Romantic.** This is generally the softer side of talking about the two of you, with specific emphasis on her. This confirms your belief in her, how you find her attractive and the bond between you. Saying 'I love you' might be going too far if she's a three-night stand, but you might say something like, 'I love being with you' or 'I feel very comfortable/sexy/alive around you.'

- **Erotic.** This is basically verbal foreplay when you use the words to arouse her and get her heading in your direction, and maybe tip her over her own limits. You're exciting her by telling her how much she turns you on and what you would like to do to her. 'I want to kiss you all over', 'I'm going to give you a slow, sensual massage and gradually work up your body until I'm inside you . . .'

- **Dirty.** This urgent, take-me-now kind of sex talk is usually reserved for those breathless moments at office parties and suchlike, when you are grabbing a passionate 'quickie' in the toilet or the back of the works van. Phrases like, 'I want to fuck you within an inch of your life' and 'I want to suck your tits' are blunt statements of intent. Let's do it now. Clearly this kind of talk should be reserved for someone or a situation that warrants it, and not leaning across a restaurant table on a first date with a wallflower.

- **Instructional.** It's good for you to know what she wants and likes and where *precisely* to put your hand. 'Higher just an inch' could mean the difference for her between 'nice' and 'mind-blowing ecstasy'. So you need to give each other licence to say what it is that excites you. There is a tendency here to get carried away though, and sound like a schoolmaster, which is really boring and an immediate passion killer. Suggest but don't criticise: 'I'd love it if you gripped me slightly harder' is much better than 'No, you're doing it all wrong, love. Do it like this . . .' And never compare and contrast an ex-lover with your present one, as in 'Angela was brilliant. She used to . . .'

- **Noising off.** Sometimes it's not only what you say but the noises you make during lovemaking that transfer positive signals that yes, she is doing the right thing and you are feeling sublimely fantastic. Mmmmm, like you've just tasted a chocolate éclair, and ecstatic moans and groans will go a long way. Psychologists have shown how encouraging noises make us even hornier – knowing that we are doing the right thing and succeeding.

- **Fantasy talk.** We all have fantasies, and being in a verbal comfort zone, where each of you has the confidence to talk about what you like, allows you both the freedom to discuss your fantasies and releases another layer of the sex game. Once you're both talking confidently to each other, there's no stopping and you are more open about everything, which makes for a much more exciting and complete relationship.

TIP: *Avoid demeaning dirty talk that is insulting and offensive. Every woman I've ever talked to about it hates being spoken to like a cheap trailer-trash bitch. So unless she specifically asks for it, during some pre-arranged fantasy, steer clear of derogatory and uncomplimentary words and phrases like, 'Take this, you miserable bitch.' I'm sure you know what I mean.*

The art of buying lingerie for your babe

Lingerie should be an active part of your sexual repertoire in that you should know what to buy, when and where to get it. Avoid buying that horrible, cheap, crinkly lingerie that will scratch your babe, and you, to death. Always deliver the lingerie you buy in a nice box with a bow.

Luckily British women are not averse to the sport of dressing up for sex and making sex into a dramatic experience. All that lace designed to lift and separate makes for a very sensual encounter as far as we men are concerned. It allows access to private parts without being completely nude and shrouds everything interesting in mystery. It allows the imagination to run wild and desire to build to a crescendo. Good lingerie accentuates curvaceous assets while disguising and camouflaging floppy bits; it should tighten and tuck in all the right places.

Overcoming resistance

With the popularity and the demystifying of sex in every department, and the success of magazines like *Loaded* and *FHM* and the acceptance of Skin 2, Agent Provocateur, Anne Summers and even high street stores like M&S, BHS and Knickerbox, British women are not really averse to the odd session of wearing fantasy garb.

Women claim not to understand the lure of lingerie, but aren't arguing with the effect it has on their man. In hot Latin countries women wear stockings and suspenders as a matter of course because pantyhose make their bits and pieces swell.

Women complain that it's uncomfortable

OK, so it might be, but you're not asking her to wear lingerie to work, or on an 18-hour flight to Los Angeles. Half an hour is all you need. She puts it on, you take it off, she puts it back on again, you take it off ... by the time she's made it from the bathroom to the bedroom, if she hasn't forgotten how uncomfortable it is, you're doing something wrong.

Women complain that it's tarty and sleazy

Of course it is – that's why we like it, and what's wrong with that? It's not as if you're asking her to parade up and down Oxford Street in a basque, and a set of stockings and suspenders. It's for your mutual enjoyment in the privacy of your own home, or hotel room. It's your little secret, providing of course you can keep the Polaroids under lock and key.

Women complain that it's pandering to male wants

Feminists argue that they shouldn't need to dress up to please their man, which is to miss the point entirely. Firstly, sex is theatre and dressing up to play your role adds fun to the proceedings. Secondly, if you would do anything to please her, shouldn't she at least get her kit off and get into some frills and lace that stick certain bits out and keep certain bits in to please you?

Buying the stuff – Rule No.1: Size her up

First thing you need to do is find out, surreptitiously, what size she is. You can do this by taking note of the label while undressing her, or by rummaging around in her knicker drawer when she's *not* around. What does 34B actually mean? The '34' is her normal clothing size and the A, B, C (or D if she's big) is the size of the cup.

What style is she?

Who cares? Never buy lingerie for her, buy it for yourself, so concentrate on extremely sexy. If you find messing about in the frilly department of your local department store a strain, relax, take a deep breath and pretend you know what you're doing. Better still, ask one of the sales ladies to give you a few tips. Don't be shy.

Grab what you want, smile as you join the queue of attractive young women clutching their own choice of frillies, and whip out your credit card. The sales ladies are perfectly clued up and won't embarrass you. Enjoy the experience.

Once you've got them home and she's got them on, then you're on your own.

How to deal with a woman with baggage

There comes a time in every man's life when he falls in love, or at the very least 'lust', with a woman with baggage. Baggage comes in many forms – it can be an ex-lover or husband, snotty children, an overly protective mother, or a destructive history of debt or drug abuse. The cumulative effect of baggage is that it gradually undermines and erodes the relationship as the genuine reasons you were attracted to her in the first place become obstructed by nonsensical clutter. Don't panic.

Everyone has some sort of baggage but if you're unfortunate enough to fall in love with a woman with excessive baggage, then you have to honestly weigh up whether or not the relationship is worth overcoming the attendant bullshit that goes with it. Baggage generally falls into five loose categories.

1. An overprotective and omnipresent parent
This is the easiest one of the lot. Be kind, courteous, generous and polite to her folks but let them know, in no uncertain terms, that you are the man of the house. Once they start interfering with your relationship, especially with regard to things like your intentions (honourable or not), and marriage

(watch for scheming mothers), then they can seriously drive you nuts. Also, if they live nearby they can be real pests by thinking they have carte blanche to pop in every five minutes. Set out a schedule of 'visiting times' and always get them to call first. Last thing you want is Mildred proudly dropping off some of her homemade plum jam and finding her precious daughter shackled to the cooker and you giving her one from behind dressed as Spiderman. She just wouldn't understand.

2. The ex-boyfriend or ex-husband

If she's over the ex-boyfriend, fine, but if he's not over her yet and is feeling seriously jilted, you've got problems. Especially if he is of a violent disposition and is currently giving your Audi TT the once-over with his baseball bat. If you're no stranger to the physical you might try having a quiet word in his ear or getting your ugly, broken-nosed brother, who's just been released from jail for GBH, to do the same. Failing that, avoid all those places where you might meet him, and in extreme cases disappear altogether. If you live in Manchester move (with the babe) to Bath. He'll get bored eventually.

3. Snotty children

You fall in love with a babe who has children. The beauty of it is you get to road-test them before deciding whether or not to get involved. Don't try and buy them (they'll hate that) and don't try and dis their father (they'll hate that even more). Explain that you don't want to be their dad, but you do love their mum and you want to love them and look after them. If her ex is a good lad, don't be obstructive, but set mutually beneficial rules regarding visiting etc.

4. A history of alcohol abuse

This all depends on how acute the problem is. If she's been living in a cardboard box under Charing Cross bridge for two years, forget it, but alcoholics *can* be saved and she will be forever in your debt for saving her and returning her skin to the complexion of peaches and cream, her brain to a functioning organ and her looks to cherry blossom fresh. Monitor her on a weekly basis, check every hiding place in the house for bottles and avoid situations where she is prone to weaken. Remember, she has got a chronic disease.

5. A history of drug abuse

Most grown-ups over the age of 20 have had some experience of drugs and flirted with some kind of drug culture. Luckily, almost 90 per cent remain in control and many decide to move on once they grow out of their trance experience or the conspiratorial thrill of 'drug theatre' wears off. Once you are through with drugs then it's doubly irritating and disappointing when you suddenly find the babe you're keen on rolling a five skinner or chasing the dragon in your bathroom. It's such a waste of time and money. You can get them off ecstasy, dope and cocaine relatively easily, although they might sell your CD collection along the way, but when somebody tells you they are going to give up heroin, never ever believe them. And watch where you're putting your Rolex. Better still, get out and keep walking, pal.

12
Well, is this love?

Relationships are never static – they are either getting better or getting worse, depending on how well we are servicing them.

'Love is a many splendored thing' (Nat King Cole), 'What is love?' (Howard Jones), 'Addicted to love' (Robert Palmer), 'What's love got to do with it?' (Tina Turner) – they've been crooning about love or lack of it, being in it and falling out of it for years, and the entire music industry would collapse without it, but only you know what love means to you. There comes a time when you have to be brutally honest with yourself and ask, is she the right woman?

Do they pass the test?

We generally pinball or lurch from one woman to another without really investigating whether or not they are a good match or truly suitable. This is understandable given the nature of courtship. When you're in the middle of a hot snogging session with that blonde from Accounts, you couldn't care less whether she's a good match or not – you can deal with that tomorrow. Right now your main concern is unhooking her bra strap.

We all tend to connect on a superficial level and then dig deeper as the relationship progresses, but there are many crucial questions that get ignored until it is way too late. Once you've passed through the favourite movie, food and music level then there are certain key areas that you will need to agree on if you are to continue to develop a healthy relationship.

Ten things you need to know

This may sound a trifle schoolmarmish, and you can't quite sit her down with what amounts to an exam paper, but consider the following ten hot topics and how they relate to her.

1. **Alcohol and smoking.** What's her attitude to both? Does she drink and if so how much? Is she a complete piss head or just a social drinker? Or is she disapproving of any sort of alcohol? And where's that bottle of ten-year-old malt that was on the sideboard last night? Alcohol is the oil that keeps many a man's wheels turning. If she drinks or smokes and you don't, or vice versa, then there's trouble ahead.

2. **Health.** Has she, or her family, got any hideous disease history you should know about? For instance, if she's

got polycystic ovaries, then she might not be able to have children. If her mother dropped dead of a heart-attack or developed diabetes at 35 then there's a good chance that she might. Has she ever had any STDs? Suffered from depression? Tried to commit suicide? What you don't want is to come home from work and find her on the window ledge because the milk's off. Does she need any expensive medication often to ward off some hideous disease?

3. **Drugs.** This subject is often shrouded in secrecy, although you should find out pretty quickly what her drug status is. A woman on drugs is not difficult to detect. One minute she's fine and the next she's agitated, fidgety, talking in tongues and enjoying watching the rubber plant grow, giggling infectiously at nothing and craving chocolate. If she starts suggesting last-minute trips to Pakistan and Thailand – this friend of a friend just happened to give her a pair of tickets – or swallowing condoms full of white powder on your annual jaunt to Majorca, you're in big trouble.

4. **Children.** I've never met a woman yet who doesn't want to have her own children at some stage. Do you? And if so when do you see yourself having them? The accepted no-risk cut-off for a woman to have children is around the 35 mark and you will find that for women over 30 the biological clock is ticking louder by the minute. This is a big thing for a woman. Yes, there are thousands of illegitimate or underage births which gives the impression that falling pregnant is easy, but consider this: it will take her a year at least to find the right guy and determine that he is the right father for her child, it might take another year for her to get pregnant,

especially if she has been on the pill for years, and then it will be nearly another year before the birth. It is a huge process. Consequently, there are plenty of single, 30-something women out there who are looking for a baby-maker.

> **NOTE:** *Know this, once you have a baby your sex life takes a serious dip.*

5. **Marriage.** Has she been married before? Does she consider this a possibility and if so in what timescale? She could be marching you up the aisle after your first kiss. Does she need to be married before you have sex? What is her parental pressure level? Do they want her out of the house? What kind of wedding does she have in mind – a Hollywood-style bash for 500 or a quiet ceremony and wild after-party?

6. **Religion.** Problem here is that many people have become so relaxed about their religious roots and claim that it doesn't really feature on their radar when actually, it does. 'It isn't an issue,' they say, which is fine until it really matters and some archaic rule or law throws a spanner in the works. Is she or has she ever been part of any religious cult? You don't want to get two months into a relationship and find that she's committed 10 per cent of your earnings to some bearded, flip-flop-wearing Indian charlatan in purple robes. Or her parents are devoted Seventh-Day Adventists and you have to give up alcohol.

7. **Sex.** Luckily it is rare now that a couple will head down any relationship road without first having sex. So the chances are that after the second or third date with a

woman you will already have a good sense of her attitudes to sex, a rough idea of her ability and experience, and an inkling of what she likes and dislikes. Does she like sex and if so how often? Is her libido healthy or would she rather be knitting? Has she got any weird fetishes or requests you can help her with or fantasies she needs realising? What's her opinion on pornography? What are her personal limits – oral sex, anal sex, group sex? You don't want to come home from the football and find her at it on the kitchen floor with your cleaning lady. Or maybe you do.

8. **Money.** Has she got any, and if not does she want money and if so how much? Are her parents poor or loaded or somewhere in between? Does she have expensive tastes? For example, when you go out does she order a gin and tonic or a magnum of crystal champagne? Does she shop for clothes at Chanel or Next or the local flea market? Does she expect you to pay for everything for the rest of your life or is she happy to chip in?

   Is she used to, and does she expect, gifts on a daily basis? What does she consider an appropriate gift for her birthday – a bottle of perfume or a handcrafted pair of Bulgari diamond earrings set in rolled platinum? Nothing less?

9. **Dreams.** Are her dreams realistic and in line with her looks, her background, her education and her talent? If she's 40, the star of the Bristol Amateur Dramatic Society and still thinks that she is going to be discovered by some roving Hollywood scout, I'll tell you right now: it is never going to happen. If she's a truly talented 22-year-old fashion designer from Halifax with no family

money, but aspires to living in a penthouse flat in New York, overlooking Washington Square, then she'd better get designing – sharpish.

You can spend an inordinate amount of time pandering to a woman's idea of who she thinks she is and where she should be. Clearly, if she can make the grade, fine, but this dream-searching can turn out to be a complete waste of time if her dreams are out of whack with her potential. And once she realises she's never going to make it, the fallout can be catastrophic.

10. **Is she who she says she is?** The latest craze in New York is to stick the name of a prospective partner in the Google search engine and see what comes up. Another device women are using is to get a private detective to check whether a man is who he says he is, does what he says he does and owns what he says he owns. This may sound a trifle excessive and obsessive but these services are also open to men to check on their women. Given that women are far less devious than men with regard to bigamy, affairs, crime and personal vices like whoring, gambling and drinking, then this may seem like a cautionary safety net too far for a man to indulge in, but you can never be sure. Chances are, if the woman you fancy is hot, and currently taking her panties off for you, then you couldn't care less if she is really an alien life form who has taken the body of a human. Whatever, or whoever, she says she is, is good enough for you.

Should you stay or should you go?

The way in which we fall into and out of relationships is haphazard, illogical, and governed more by fate and good timing than forward planning. But that's part of what makes relationships magical. Once you're in one, a relationship takes on its own rhythm and it becomes increasingly difficult to break free of it the longer it goes on. Even relationships that aren't necessarily made in heaven work to a point because those locked in to them are too lazy, too settled or too immersed in joint plans to ever break out of them and search for that ultimate relationship that will make them truly happy. So if you're bored with what you've got but can't get off your fat ass long enough to find somebody new, then stop complaining – you've only yourself to blame.

But how do you know when she's the right woman and how right is right? Relationships are never static – they are either getting better or getting worse, depending on how well we are servicing them.

The big question is: is your relationship good and getting better, and are you in this relationship for the long haul or the short term? Why trundle along in a relationship that isn't going anywhere when you could be in a completely fulfilling relationship that's going everywhere you ever wanted it to? How do you know?

The *Right Woman, Right Now* 'Love-ometer'

If you answer 'yes' to more than six of the following questions (and be honest now), then you are definitely in love with her.

1. Do you think you are in love with her?
2. Do you want to be in love with her?
3. Do you want her to be in love with you?
4. Have you found the woman of your dreams?
5. Have you stopped looking for somebody better?
6. Would you marry this woman?

7. Would you have children with this woman?
8. If she left you tomorrow would you be devastated?
9. When she isn't around do you pine for her?
10. Is she your best friend?

How to Give Her Absolute Pleasure
Totally explicit techniques every woman wants her
man to know
Lou Paget
0 7499 2262 1

'Every man who wants to satisfy his woman should study this
wonderfully informative book.'
Bernie Zilbergeld, author of *The New Male Sexuality*

Here is a sex guide written especially for men. Men are expect-
ed to 'just know' how to please a woman, and women are often
reluctant to say what they really want. This refreshingly frank
and explicit handbook gives you all the information you need.
Packed full of steamy tips and little-known techniques and
tricks, it is guaranteed to drive her wild.

Lou Paget is one of America's most popular 'sexperts' and an
experienced sex educator. She is the author of the acclaimed
sex guide for women, *How to Be a Great Lover*. She has run
sell-out Sexuality Seminars since 1993 and writes regularly for
Cosmopolitan, *Glamour* and *Playboy*.